Is It Just Me?
Or
Everyone a Little Nuts!

Judi Coltman

In the interest of full disclosure, some names and places may have been changed. . .but then again, maybe not.

ISBN 978-0-557-56654-9

I have parents who cheer for me. I have friends who encourage me. I have a husband and kids who lift me up.

They all make me laugh and allow me to love.

This is for you all!

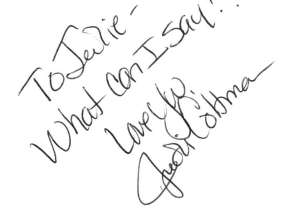

Foreword

"You should be a writer," words often uttered in my ear by well-meaning people even when I was writing for local and national publications. "You should publish a book." Oh, ok - why didn't I think of that? Like I could just sit down and write and magically it becomes a book? "You should write that story down, it was hysterical."

Guess what!

I did.

Chapter One

Where Yat?

I am directionally challenged. I cannot get anywhere by following the cardinal directions. I require landmarks.

When we first moved to Northern Illinois in 1983, the only place we could find for rent was in the smallest town in the world (population 600, which rapidly headed up to 602.) We lived in a duplex on Elm Street, not that anyone needed to know that because we had to go to the Post Office to collect the mail (P.O. Box 12.) The Smallest Town in the World had, at that time, its own telephone company, a bar, the Good Food cafe and Henry's Royal Blue store where you could buy groceries, hardware and carpet. It is impossible to not know where something is in The Smallest Town in the World. It's either up by the school, out by the old Chicken's Roost or in town. The Smallest Town in the World is 7 miles west of the thriving metropolis which we escaped to only a year later.

The Thriving Metropolis sits on the Rock River in a strange jog that goes east and west even though the river generally runs north and south. That being said, direction has tripped me up since we first came to town. I will tell you all day long that the highway that hugs the river runs north to south and all day long it will really run east and west. Thankfully, that is not necessary information to retain because no one here knows how to give directions to anything that entails the compass rose.

It's true. I have a friend who is moving from her home on the river (known as the River House) to a neighborhood called Brighton Ridge. "Where?" Almost EVERYONE who asks asks. The new neighborhood at the top of Hill Road by the water tower and across from Snapke's. . . .ohhhhh come knowing nods. The mention of Snapke's Farm that has now been encroached by "urban sprawl" always clarifies the location, which is funny because Snapke's left the farm years ago.

My friend Nel lives in Nikki's old house. Peg lives in Nikki's other old house. Nikki's new house is out by the old Haskin's Farm which means we all seem to know where Nikki has lived. I'm not really sure how or why Nikki's houses have attained landmark status so don't ask.

I'm fairly positive that the reason delivery businesses use GPS these days is because of how I give directions. I could always envision the facial reaction of whatever poor soul had to deliver something to my house. . .and get directions from me as I spoke. I am sure they were mouthing the word "DITZ!!" to whomever was around:

Take the Highway toward Dixon. As you come into town you will pass a brand new medical building on your left. It's abandoned. Then you will pass the sewage treatment plant. Welcome to Metropolis. At the first light Union Street Station will be on your right. Yes, it's for sale, but it has been since I moved here and it won't hinder the annual Turkey Testicle Festival in October. Keep going past the town clock in Fountain Park and the library will be on your right. . .and on your left. But if you really want to know, it used to be in the Community Center (upstairs); a preschool (downstairs) and is now the Heavenly Glory Church. The new old library building is for sale, but we have a brand new library that is across the highway on your left that has been aptly named The High Rise but pales in comparison to the architectural vision of our school district leader (and I know she lays awake at night gnashing her teeth over the whole affair.) Keep going to the third light (and really 3 stop lights in Metropolis is an occurrence over the last 5 years) at Hill Road. There's a Family Video on the right that shut down two locally owned video stores in town (and ok, who really rents videos anymore) but it's fine because only one of those buildings is for sale. Then there is The Dog 'n Suds Drive-In. Yes, they really do still exist and it is a teenage girl's right of passage to car hop there for at least one summer of her life. So, drive past Cal's Barber & Used Car Shop and start looking at the roads on the right. I live at the corner of Main and Pine across from the Farr's and next to where Abe Swenson used to live with his sister Frances. Our house used to have a flagpole but we removed it. I still believe that we are good Americans.

Still, it's a whole lot easier now that I live back in the Metropolis after a stint of country living. Imagine me having to give directions to my house on Raccoon Trail in Oregon (the town, not the state) even though I had a Metropolis phone number, paid taxes to Metropolis and schooled my kids in Metropolis instead. To make matters worse, there are TWO Raccoon Trails in Oregon that are not connected and have similar house numbers five miles apart. Take that, GPS! Suddenly, traveling by way of landmark doesn't seem so ditzy, does it?

Chapter Two

Would You Take A Dime?

Against my better judgement and admonishments from friends, I found myself sitting at a garage sale yesterday - all day. At least I had the foresight to piggyback on someone else's sale at someone else's house, but the pain is still the same.

In an effort to ward off the people who circle the house like hawks two hours before you open at 8 a.m. and pounce on you as you carry things into the driveway or (and yes, this has happened) CRAWL UNDER THE GARAGE DOOR before you have a chance to haul out the money box and then have the audacity to offer you a dime for something marked 25 cents. . .we opened at 4 p.m. Wednesday.

What time did the first visitor make his way down the driveway? 2:30 p.m.! He knew that a) it was early, b) I didn't have change yet c) the house where we are having the garage sale has, itself, been for sale (the River House, in fact) and d) we were still marking items.

I was the only one there at the time and this guy asks if the house is still for sale. I tell him there is an offer and a closing date and then he asks me, HOW MUCH DID I

GET!?! I tell him I don't live there, but I ask you, what kind of person asks that kind of question? I was stunned. Then, he peruses the tables, picking things up, carrying them around and laying them in another spot. Finally he picks up my friend's camera that is sitting on a table next to me and asks,"How much?" I VERY POLITELY (because my mother taught me well) reach for the camera and tell him it isn't for sale. Early bird customer pulls it away from me and says, "You should do a walk through before you let people in and end up HAVING to sell things you didn't intend to."
WHAT???

Needless to say, I got the camera and the man left after purchasing some books (for which he tried to offer half the total of $3.) Well friends, the beauty of small-town living is this: I figured out who the man was and were I a more vindictive soul, would print the name here.

Thank goodness there is a natural balance in the world because yesterday, an apparent stroke victim in her mid 50's appeared and very carefully kept counting her change as she considered clothing items. Then, she stopped in her tracks and gushed, GUSHED at a painting I had out. It was a canvas where I was experimenting with transfer techniques and, honestly, I didn't really care for it. If nothing else, I figured someone could buy the canvas, cover over it and do their own thing. She weighed her need for the clothes against her desire for the painting and opted for the clothes. I weighed my desire for a few extra bucks against the opportunity to make someone's day. I gave her the painting. I helped her to her car (there was a driver waiting) and she hugged me - which is not an activity I usually engage in with strangers - I'm not even thrilled about touching the money that people hand me, but it felt right.

I think next time I feel the need to eliminate "things" - I'll bypass the bad karma of a garage sale and donate it all to the hospice resale shop. Then, I won't have to worry about counting dimes.

CHAPTER THREE

FIVE THINGS I SIMPLY REFUSE TO DO:

I consider myself a pretty good sport about most things. I once, in the interest of new love, braved an activity I never engaged in as a child and only willingly complied because there were big, mean dogs going along to protect us. That activity? Camping. I don't mean the clean kind of camping where there is a campsite, showers and restrooms. I mean the kind of camping where we ate canned Chef Boyardee spaghetti that was so vile, the dogs wouldn't finish it. I mean the kind of camping where large snakes sought out our body heat and curled up next to our sleeping bags, driving me to run screaming for the refuge of the backseat of a Pontiac Sunbird. I mean the kind of camping that required a walk in the woods to find a private tree to squat over that wasn't infested with biting bugs or carpeted in poison ivy. And just so you know. . .I found the poison ivy.

It's taken years for me to shed the activities for which I no longer wish to partake. I no longer camp. Ever. I don't do yard work. I don't take out the trash. And there are a few others things I just don't feel like doing anymore. I figure, why keep it a secret?

1) **Work for my food** - I love shrimp, but I am not peeling it, pulling off it's tail or head and I am NOT removing the mud vein. And why do they call it a mud vein? Who do they think they are fooling? We all know what it really is and, I'm not meddling with it.

2) **Touch a Snake** - Nope. There is no reasoning here either. Whatever you do, do not try to entice me to see how friendly the serpent really is by approaching me with it in hand because I will hyper ventilate, pass out cold and when I come to, I will kill you.

3) **Go Commando** - Say what you will about the virtues of going without underwear, I'm not buying it. Nothing sounds more uncomfortable than having the thick denim crotch of blue jeans rubbing my naughty bits. It spells blisters and ooze. No thanks. I'll stick with my grandma panties.

4) **Swim in a Public Pool** - We all have our "ick" factors. Well, mine is public water. Specifically, public pools. The thought makes me sudder with disgust. It doesn't matter where it is or how clean it seems, if I go into a pool that caters to many others, the floating clump of hair, tossed aside baggie and abandoned bandaid will find me. Going to the local water park? I'll be the dry one sitting on my little island of lounge chair paradise.

5) **Look at My Reflection from Anywhere but Head On**- My mom never understood how I could leave the house without combing the hair on the back of my head. Here's why: If you aren't in my direct frontal view, chances are good I am not engaging you in any way, ergo, I don't need to impress you. Also, any other angle on my body is just plain unattractive. I had the misfortune of catching a glimpse of my side view the other day that rendered me stricken with horror and asking, "Who in the hell put that ass on my butt?"

As I steadily march on to my next year of life, I will, assuredly, uncover more things I simply refuse to do and you can bet I'll let you know about them.

Chapter Four

Her? She's My Cousin

I was a Cub Scout den mother. There, I said it. This is critical information key to understanding the story I am about to tell. My best friend Darling Deb and I were co-leaders for our sons' cub scout den. I came to it by virtue of a moment of insanity and anger when I realized I could not complain about the way an organization was run unless I was willing to step in to facilitate a change. For the record, this occurred about the time I had read Steven Covey's, *Seven Habits of Highly Successful People* and was feeling empowered by my "roles" and personal mission statement which long ago got buried by the myriad corpses of self improvement books and plans, diet books and exercise videos.

Not only was I a leader but, in my zeal to make a change, I was the Pack secretary to whom the responsibility of planning large Pack activities and correspondences fell upon. And so it was, I was the designated writer of **the** letter in response to our Chamber of Commerce's sudden refusal to pay an agreed upon sum for services provided during our town's big summer event, Summerfest.

Summerfest equates to one big drunkfest during the weekend after the 4th of July. With three separate stages featuring bands from throughout the midwest, two adjoining beer gardens, the Taste area for food and a carnival among the slew of activities scheduled for the weekend, it is a mega money maker for our little city and requires a town full of volunteers to pull off. One of the fundraisers for our Pack was a clean-up crew, made up of parents, that showed up Saturday and Sunday mornings bright and early to clean up the beer garden areas. A deal had been struck between a scout "official" and a crony from the chamber whereby they would pay $500 to the Pack in exchange for morning clean-up services all weekend. This deal was made in the early years of Summerfest, but with the influx of new people and attrition of the scouts and their parents. . .those players were no longer in the game. And being a small town, the Pack continued to fulfill their portion of the deal until we received "The Letter." When "The Letter" arrived a month after Summerfest, we opened it with anticipation only to find a check for $50 and an explanation. Basically and eloquently written by the Chamber Representative, who, I am sure was directed to word it with a kind firmness, it simply stated:

Please find enclosed a check for $50 for services rendered during Summerfest. After a meeting to discuss disbursement, we agreed on this sum for several reasons. . . .blah, blah, blah. And finally, we did not see any of your fine young men on either morning working

to clean the area in any capacity. Therefore, please accept this check and we thank you for all your work over the years.
Sincerely,

The Chamber Rep.

Directed by the Pack Leader to send a letter of "thanks" back to the chamber, I penned the following:

Dear Ms. Chamber Rep.,
Thank you for your generous yet disappointing check of $50. Being a service-oriented group that attempts to teach our boys the virtues of honesty and hard work, we are grateful for any opportunity to raise funds for Pack activities. Perhaps you are new to this community? It has always been the practice of our Pack to raise funds through adult services. Ergo, we have never sent our fine young men into the beer gardens of Summerfest the morning after to clean up. We do not feel that an environment that promotes public drunkenness and urination into the wee hours of the morning, nor the grounds covered with vomit, used prophylactics, and discarded underwear is an environment conducive to raising well-adjusted boys. Blab, blah, blah niceties and heartfelt thanks.

Very truly yours,
Judi Coltman
Cub Scout Pack Secretary

Stuck it to them, didn't I?

I got a down and dirty, gut-wrenching, butt clenchingly deep satisfaction writing it - in several different versions each one nastier than the last and I pictured the intended recipient reading it, pursing her lips, and getting all flustered. It was a vision that elicited a continuous genuine joy until about three years ago.

Three years ago, in a serendipitous mix of fleet-footed ability, I became friends with two incredibly kind people whose son ran with my son to a State track medal. Proud beaming parents we, gushing over the remarkable ability of our progeny and, thus; became friends. Pretty darn good friends. Who are they? Yeah, you guessed it-- Ms. Chamber Rep. and her husband. She's never said a word about it. Now that's class.

In this town, the ubiquitous 6 Degrees of Separation is really only 1.5 and everyone is someone's cousin. It pays to talk nice because the person you blast may become one of your best friends!

Chapter Five

Dan Brown Could Learn A Thing or Two

I have a group of friends here in town that I adore beyond words. Actually I have several groups of friends that I adore beyond words because that is the nature of small towns. This particular group, however, never ceases to disappoint. We all worked together at the school in very different capacities but were drawn to one another like magnets, we believe, due to our engaging personalities, intellectual prowess, and blinding beauty. We are a fascinating group - the type of social group everyone would want to be a part of if they realized what fun we have. . .or that we even exist. We call ourselves, "The Planning Committee."

The Planning Committee first convened, ostensibly, to plan a Bunco gathering, put together a schedule of dates and get the dice rolling *so to speak*. What happened at that meeting, well, it stays at that meeting but I can tell you that we consumed mass quantities of wine and Seagram's drinks, laughed until our stomach's hurt (which all agreed constitutes multiple sets of stomach crunches) and our eyes burned with tears. Forget Bunco

- we decided to leave that for the less imaginative people who needed an activity to justify a get together. We had more fun "planning," thus; The Planning Committee was established.

And guess what! It was the best cover EVER. We could talk about getting together in front of others without hurting the feelings of those others simply by saying the words, "planning" and "committee." Everyone else just assumed we were planning some kind of school function. So official sounding was The Planning Committee, we could announce on the PA system throughout the entire school that an emergency meeting of The Planning Committee would be taking place at my house, or The Fifth or Tailgaters and no one would even question it. That, by the way, would fall under "intellectual prowess."

And so we would gather and talk with NOTHING being out of bounds. And, oh my, the things we know about each other and our spouses! The thing is, on our own, we are amazing enough but as a group we are freakin' magnificent.

We have the wife of a Healthcare CEO who makes me laugh like a sister-- in fact, we told many a student that we are sisters. The gal holds NOTHING back delivering her quips with a ferocity that would make Joy Behar blush.

We have two townie originals who, between them, can connect every person in town to each other and no one needs Kevin Bacon to round it out. They know the town secrets and share them liberally, which means we know way more than anyone should about the average citizen. But we have pinky sworn never to divulge unless, of course, someone pisses us off.

We have probably the nicest person to ever walk this earth. She shoulders the responsibility of the world's ills without martyrdom and then, while juggling said ills will utter the snarkiest, funniest comment I have ever heard punctuated with an F-Bomb or two all without missing a beat and maintaining the juggle when anyone else would have dropped it all. In short, I call her the Salt of the Earth.

And we have a level-headed, wise, thoughtful and well read Michigan State University graduate who is SO grounded that she could handle something as unbelievable as becoming a grandmother when NO ONE including family members who are doctors realized a birth was pending. That's another story all together. . .but it ends with the most beautiful, healthy 8 pound baby boy and surprised parents who have embraced their new role. In short, we have among us enough knowledge and secrets to make any society Dan Brown writes about seem like child's play.

This particular committee member, Bea, is a plant miracle worker and has a backyard that includes, an english garden, wild flowers and a sweeping prairie. It's amazing. If she touches a plant, it blooms. If she talks to a tomato it grows and her yard attracts butterflies of all types and blue birds - which were endangered. The truth is, Bea makes Snow White look like a poser.

And it's the elusive Blue Bird, I have found, that tipped our even handed Bea to introduce us to her evil side - the one that finds the idea of murder a perfectly acceptable form of punishment.

You see, Bea was delighted when she discovered that Blue Birds had found the house built and placed specially for them. She enjoyed the addition and checked on them often. The blue birds, in turn flitted around her as she walked and I swear they laid a garland of flowers over her shoulders. So you can imagine her disappointment when she happened upon the Blue Bird house one day and found that it had been invaded by sparrows who had, in a siege, killed her beloved Blue Birds. Bea was not happy, and rest assured, was not going to allow THAT to happen again. Bea bided her time all summer and stewed about it through the fall and winter. By spring, she knew how to handle the situation should it occur again.

Sure enough, Blue Birds returned to the house and Bea kept a constant eye on it . . .waiting for the marauders to appear and roust out her Blue Birds. And, they did. Level-headed Bea knew there was only one thing to do to protect the Blue Birds, their nest and any unhatched Blue Birds to be. Bea kept a constant vigil, waiting until she saw the sparrow enter the bird house. Then, she snuck up behind the bird house and threw a trash bag over the house, pounded on the house to scare the sparrow out, catching it in the garbage bag, tightened the opening and removed the sparrow from the house. But now what to do? If she let it go, it might come back. If she left it in the bag, it might rip its way out. . .so she decided, not without a small bit of pleasure, that a quick in end was in order.

Opening the bag enough to slip it over the tailpipe of her RUNNING car, she retied it tightly and then revved the engine a few times. . . for the fun of it.

Well you can guess the rest. What's frightening is not that murder was the only way she saw fit to correct the situation, but the fact that she thought about the MODE of murder long enough to be creative about the whole thing. Snow White's wicked queen's got nothing on Bea and at this point I'm not sure I'd accept an apple from Bea either. Sure, she eradicated the killer sparrows saving the Blue Birds to thrive but I'm thinking that if other neighborhood pets come up missing we know where to look first! HOWEVER and here is the caveat: We will NOT admit that to anyone - EVER. We protect our own. We are the Planning Committee. We will throw ourselves under the party bus to uphold the secret (unless it is going to ruin our cute shoes) even if it is a little creepy.

[Editing Note: When Salt of the Earth read this article she pulled me aside and said, " I loved what you wrote about Bea!" So I asked what she thought about her description. Her response? "I didn't realize I was in it."]

CHAPTER SIX

WHEN IN ROME

Growing up in the suburbs of Detroit, the 4th of July was a day where we planned some kind of family outing to mark the glory of independence. That would include the Detroit River fireworks extravaganza, a Pop's concert at Meadowbrook Hall and finally the "Guess who Drove to Canada and Smuggled Back Illegal Fireworks" show which always occurred when most of the world was heading to bed.

A few pops, sizzles and pows later, our backdoor neighbor, Jack, would come barreling through the bushes that divided our properties threatening to call the police. Jack, whom we always called Jackpot due to a beer belly that would make a 3rd trimester pregnant woman proud, liked a cocktail. He was a staunch high school principal by day, but by 5 p.m., Jackpot was letting his hair down. By midnight, he loved everyone and everything and all he really wanted to do was light off a bottle rocket or two.

Dick would show up moments into the show carrying his British flag and a whole cadre of his own illegal fireworks, "To show you chaps that we really are still in charge!" And the grown-males-behaving-like-ten-year-old-boys hijinks ensued, usually with the cops making a few passes in front of the house and ending with the adults hiding in Jackpot's cabana giggling wildly while we kids swam in the pool until 2 a.m. telling the officer standing at the pool gate, "Why yes, we saw someone was shooting off fireworks but we have no idea who. . . ."

Those were the "Big City" days. Now, my 4th of July's are spent in Mt. Morris, Illinois. The parade starts at 1 p.m. with people staking their claim along the parade route the night before - setting up chairs and spreading blankets. Remarkably, other people respect this process and no one's stuff gets taken or even moved!

The Mt. Morris parade is a really LONG parade lasting a good hour and it is never complete without the Shriner's zipping by in their airplane 3 wheelers, threatening to mash the toes of those in the way. The Shriner's do a lot of good with their hospital programs but they do even better in the parade arena. They come complete with their own keg equipped bus that follows behind them in the parade, collects them at the end and ushers them off to their next gig. . .while they work on draining the keg. The number of parades scheduled before Mt. Morris determines just how drunk they are when they whiz by us. It's a known and accepted given; Get Jimmy off the street and away from the curb, the Shriner's have been to 3 parades already!

The tried and true sign that the parade is coming to an end are the horses. When the various riding clubs, ranches and miniature horse breeders come through, it's your signal to stand up. The final entrant is the manure wagon which is pulled by two kids while two more shovel up the horse pies and throw them in the wagon. No one leaves until the manure wagon has passed and you have offered appropriate applause to the kids who are shoveling the poop.

As the sky begins to darken, you can hear the faint strains of the Mt. Morris "Let Freedom Ring" band playing at the school football field; a signal that it's time to head up there for fireworks. The entire football field and surrounding grounds is packed with families from small towns all over the area seated on blankets or lawn chairs. As the band strikes up the "Star Spangled Banner," everyone stands, then the vehicle carrying the "Let Freedom Ring" queen and her attendants ferries the beauties around the track as the queen waves to her people. Little girls watch in awe as they imagine that someday it might be them while little boys run around with sparklers or toss footballs. But, when the first report of the fireworks is heard, everyone settles down, lying on their backs to watch the most spectacularly colorful display of fireworks ever blossoming in the sky.

I sometimes miss those days where I wondered whether we would be hiding from the cops but it's nice to NOT worry about getting arrested for a change.

Chapter Seven

You Can't Find The Answers Until You Know How to Ask The Questions

Having worked in our school district full time, raised two kids who both finished school (genuflect) and subbed in three other districts. . .one thing stands clear; you can pretty much gauge a child's educational enjoyment level by their first formal schooling experience. Ergo, I'd rate the kindergarten teacher as possibly the most influential person your child will encounter in the first ten years of his or her little life.

My oldest had a perfect match in his kindergarten teacher. I remember being floored by the amount of effort she put into every word she spoke and how she made it correlate with what was being learned. You may think it was just natural communication but her phrases were peppered with the sound that was being taught at every turn. And quite frankly, it must have been exhausting.

My youngest had a similarly positive experience with a different teacher who was a perfect fit. I had the pleasure of getting to know VW (as she is known around these parts) as his kindergarten teacher first, but as a colleague several years later. VW had a brilliant sense of humor and found humor in her students as well and thus, joy. You could tell when VW was on a roll telling a story, her signature laugh bellowed down the halls and drew most of us to where she was because, by God, VW was telling a story. One of my FAVORITE VW stories involves a student named Bobby.

Bobby, as a kindergartener had a mad crush on a pretty little girl named Samantha. He was convinced that someday he was going to marry her and boldly shared that notion with anyone who would listen.. .many times over. . .day after day. At recess one day, Bobby discovered that another little boy also had a crush on Samantha . Bobby was NOT happy with this prospect (a scoundrel out to ruin his plans) so the first chance he got when the no one was looking, he pushed this boy to the ground and told him to go find his own wife. The boy who, like any kindergartener would. . .told the recess monitor.

When class was over, the recess monitor, marched Bobby back to the classroom. " Mrs. VW, I think you need to know that Bobby pushed another little boy at recess today. " VW feigning utter shock turned to Bobby and asked why he would do such a thing. Bobby just hung his head. The recess monitor explained that this other little boy said HE was going to marry little Samantha and Bobby just could not cotton to that so he pushed the boy. Without skipping a beat , VW looked at Bobby and scolded, "Bobby! How many times have I told you that you CANNOT GET MARRIED until you learn how to read!" Bobby pitifully hung his head and mumbled, "OoooooKayyyyy, I'm sorry."

That was the great thing about VW. She allowed that all kids were different. They acted different, they grew different and they learned different. VW embraced that in her students, encouraging them to find their strengths and grow. I remember sitting at my first parent-teacher conference with her. I was concerned whether my child could recognize the letter W. Mary VW looked at me, laughed her signature laugh and said, "Relax. That kid has a whole bunch of questions bottled up inside him that he is just dying to get the answers to. He'll learn the W when he's ready to ask the questions."

She was right. The questions are still coming.

It is necessary to note that this wonderful teacher recently passed away after an iron-willed battle with cancer. With her daughters at her side and a steady stream of teacher friends to visit with, Mary kept them all laughing as she slowly died. She was a teacher of children, she was a teacher to teachers, she was a teacher to her friends and she taught us all about happiness.

Chapter Eight

But Wait, There's More

Show of hands and be honest; how many of you have been pulled into an infomercial and found yourself actually considering the wondrous possibilities of [insert favorite product here]? Uh huh, that's what I thought. . .me too.

I don't really remember watching Ron Popeil hawk his famous Pocket Fisherman, but I do know that he formed Ronco, and was the inventor of the following amazing products: The Chop-o-Matic, Veg-o-Matic, In the Eggshell Scrambler, and Hair in a Can, among others. I myself first became mesmerized by the 5 Tray Food Dehydrator. I mean really, you can dry fruit and store it in an airtight package (see Seal a Meal, now available at stores near you) or make your own beef jerky by simply putting it in the dehydrator. Never mind that sometimes it did not completely dry the food. What's a little mold between friends?

I have never personally succumbed to the "Act Now" message of the infomercial hawker. Not even the late Billy Mays could persuade me to call in the next 10 minutes, no matter what they included at three simple payments of $29.99.

But guess what I found recently at a mall in Michigan? A genuine, real and true store called "As Seen On TV." Yes folks, there it was in all its glory situated right between Eddie Bauer and Victoria's Secret! And like moths to the "Insecterator", I was drawn in. And, oh my, they had it all: The Snuggie; the mini-blind cleaner; the Bedazzler; the Ab Rocket; Sham WOW; Hollywood Bump Its and those miracle bra clip thingies.

It's easy when you have a TV screen as a buffer between you and the amazing product. It's a whole different game when the products are there for trying before you buy. And try, I did. While the Ab Rocket was tempting, I wasn't sure I had any room next to the Ab Lounger and the all-in-one gym in our basement storage area. Pass. Sham WOW? Pass. BEDAZZZZZZZZLER? Hmmmm. Pass. There was the Space Bag with the new vacuum technology straight from NASA for safe storage of your fine sweaters, The Green Bag that guarantees that your vegetables and fruits will last 10 days longer than regularly stored veggies (and you get 3 bonus bags!); and the Buxton Bag, the purse guaranteed to organize even the most disheveled individual. This fantastic bag included a pocket ON THE STRAP just for your cell phone. My heart be still. Imagine all of the space, grocery money and time I can save with just these three simple bags. But wait. . . suddenly there was a glow coming from across the store like a golden neon arrow saying "Try This." And I was drawn away from the amazing bags and off to another section of the store. I swear that there was an undertone of, "oooooooohhhs and ahhhhhhhs" embedded in the Muzak. The answer to all of my problems was before me for one low price.

The next time you see me in town please feel free to tell me how darn good I look as I will be sporting my new Hollywood Bump It in my hair and the bra clip thingy on my bra making my posture more erect and the girls less saggy. All of this for the one low price of $18.99. And if you want to know how well these products really work, just mail me three separate payments of $9.99 and I'll send you my own personal analysis of said products with directions on how to get to that store.

Now I'd like to get my hands on that new curling iron with the spinning barrel. Or how about the red thing that bakes cakes in minutes. Maybe a . . .

CHAPTER NINE

SERENDIPITY

Disclaimer: I am in California as I write this. This is necessary information that has absolutely nothing to do with the following piece but to let you know that it is sunny and warm and I don't want to come home.

When I was very young, I was addicted to "The Patty Duke" show. Patty and her cousin Cathy (they were cousins, identical cousins) were my quintessential ideal of "teenager." By age four I had mastered Patty speak and was called upon by my parents to utter a Patty inspired, "Bye E" when saying goodbye to guests who then departed in snickers and giggles.

As I got older, I traded Patty in for the Sally Field incarnation of Gidget. Where Patty Duke was my childhood vision of teenager, Gidget was my tween ideal. Who couldn't love a girl with that name?

Gidget loved music, hung out at the beach (that sealed the deal right there for me) and had a surfer boyfriend named Moondoggy. Moondoggy was a goofy character, but I thought he was dreamy. And he surfed! Moondoggy taught me what a teenage girl's boyfriend should be. He was attentive, he was willing to be the Ethel to Gidget's Lucy and he was respectful of Gidget's befuddled and distrusting single father. What more could a girl ask for (the mother in me answers that with, " Earning Potential", but my Gidget persona wasn't thinking of that at 16.)

So, my secret is out. My alter ego is named Gidget and she surfaces more often than you would think. Further, Gidget grew up and married Moondoggy (Ok, not the REAL Moondoggy, but don't tell my spouse, he doesn't know.) Life is good.

On my early morning walk today, I was deep into thought about what I might do when I grow up when someone sneezed right behind me startling me back into the moment. I must have jumped pretty high and had the look of fear written across my face because, the sneezer was immediate to respond with kindness and care. "Are you ok? I am so sorry, I get deep into my head too, is your heart pounding?" He reached out and touched my shoulder as we stood at the intersection waiting for the "Walk" sign. He was a runner. He had sun bleached blond hair that reminded me of Owen Wilson, a little wild, but not too long. He wore orange and red board shorts in a length conducive for running and allowing for an appreciative view of his, uh, legs. And he wore no shirt. Instead, his upper body was a study in Adonis. His hairless torso was well toned and evenly, beautifully tanned to a sun kissed California bronze. He touched my shoulder and I looked into his blue eyes. There was a look of momentary confusion followed by just a split second of recognition before the "walk" sign flashed and he ran off.

Watching him dart off ahead of me, I sighed, "Moondoggy, don't you recognize me?" But I was wearing black cotton "mom" shorts and a Walmart brand t-shirt. My hair was pinned up with bobby pins while the "old lady" hairs that gray and frizz were waving out around the edges. I didn't even have on my miracle bra clip or my spiffy new Hollywood Bump It, but I think he must have recognized me. As he ran off, he called out, "Enjoy the day, babe!" He called me "Babe" – he must have known it was me – Gidget!

CHAPTER TEN

COUGARS AND CUTE BOYS

Life has a way of keeping me humble. I am not one of those people who feel the need to deny my years, but I do sometimes feel the need to reassure myself that I have not slipped into the point of no return.

So, 48-year old me keeps a strong alliance with 17-year-old me, allowing 17-year-old me to look at "cute boys" (and I DO TRY to stay in the beyond 20 range, really I do,) while 48-year-old me tempers the thoughts with wisdom and good judgement (stop laughing!!) The first time my two "me's" merged, bestowing upon me a huge dose of humble was last summer at the beach. Seventeen-year-old me noticed a very cute boy with surfer long hair, golden tan and a contagious laugh. Seventeen-year-old me, admired the boy while 48-year-old me firmly kept my mouth from gaping open. He was so, so cute! And, as I followed his movements for the better part of two hours while I sat in my beach chair reading a book, I harkened back to my glory days when I KNEW he would have been my beach boyfriend. I did this until I noticed him approach this beautiful woman who was clearly older than he. "Yeah," I thought, "a Cougar." She gently rubbed his shoulders with sunscreen before he headed back out into the surf. As he grabbed his surf board he turned back to The Cougar, flashed that gorgeous smiled and said, "Thanks Mom!"

48-year-old me told 17-year-old-me to go take a shower. Instant humble.

But it keeps coming. My oldest child is in his twenties. He invited me down for a final Mom's Weekend at college in April where we did the "Mom Bar Crawl." At one point a large group of young men burst into the bar asking, "So where are all the cougars?????" I instantly, as I often do because I can be a smart ass, shouted back, "Over here!" and then laughed because I knew they had not heard me. . .thank goodness. Forty-eight-year old me was relieved and proud. I thought I had 17-year-old me quelled and in check - FINALLY.

Ha! Last Saturday, we were at a graduation party for the daughter of a friend. There was a DJ there playing a wide range of music but kind enough to spin "Love Shack" for the parents there and it got us all out on the dance floor. We danced, we jammed, we sang and then I looked up and made eye contact with a very cute boy standing off to the side watching the parent show. He had these sparkling eyes, a genuine smile, and hair that curled out from under his baseball cap. And. . .he was watching me. It was a little disconcerting but somewhere 17-year-old me was smiling back. When the song was over, the cute boy with the sparkling eyes yells, "Mrs. Coltman!!! I remember when you used to drive me to pre-school in carpool!"

Humbled again.

Cougar? Me? That's way more work than I'm willing to
do. I think I'd rather be an old house cat.

CHAPTER ELEVEN

WHAT'S A LITTLE CHRISTMAS NEWSLETTER BETWEEN FRIENDS?

My mother is rolling over in her grave. I did the unthinkable and she is not happy. I seriously cut down my Christmas card list this year and thus, am posting my annual newsletter as a blog. I'd like to think it's because I am deeply involved in eliminating my carbon footprint but the truth is. . .I got a cramp in my hand and don't feel like addressing envelopes anymore. Come to think of it, Emily Post isn't too happy about this either.

Happy Holidays to Everyone!
This was supposed to be THE year. The one event that every parent who has the opportunity waits for. All of our children graduated this year (all both of them.) Which meant that we would finally be facing the proverbial empty nest. And we were EXCITED! At least that was my plan. To truly describe how my plan was supposed to go down, I have to go back in time. . .

Every August from the time both of my kids were in school, we looked toward the first day of school with a mixture of excitement and dread. At least that is what the kids thought. It was hard for Oldest Son and and

Youngest Son to imagine what my pathetic little life would be like all day without their constant company. And every year, I would solemnly assure that them that I would, somehow, manage. Along with my next-door neighbor and BFF Cindy, we would slowly walk the kids to the bus stop and sadly wave our babies off into another year of school. And when the bus was safely out of site, BFF Cindy and I would allow the smiles to creep across our faces as we danced, DANCED back to our houses, put on a Springsteen CD and toasted our freedom with mimosa's and cake (Yes! Cake!)

Flash forward to the proud day this May when Oldest Son walked across the stage at the University of Illinois and into the real world. It really is something to realize that this truly is IT. At 22, Oldest had college under his belt and a job on the line. Life is good. Two weeks later, Youngest walked across the stage at the high school and into college mode heading to the University of Illinois thus, rendering our nest empty - which we were both really looking forward to. Yeah, yeah, you miss the kids and all but come on. . . .the house empties by two full people! Fewer clothes strewn around the house, one less bathroom to CONTINUALLY clean, and a grocery bill that diminishes by over HALF! Yep, that was my plan.

So, imagine my surprise when Oldest moved home at the end of July because his job with a cruise company (based in Hawaii, poor boy) would not begin until late September. There we were, all four of us in 1200 square feet. Full-time. That was not my plan.

However, I quickly found out that this arrangement came with perks! Oldest did the grocery shopping, meal planning and he did a lot of the cooking. What a gift! I could hold off on my plan for awhile.

Youngest headed off to college in mid-August, learning to navigate the city by public transportation in short order. He quickly became attuned to city life; shopping, going to concerts and the symphony. Oldest got the call to head to Hawaii to begin his job in September. I took him to the airport in the early hours of Friday, Sept. 25 knowing that I would come home to an EMPTY NEST. Imagine my surprise when, as he got out of the car and hugged me goodbye, I began to sob. SOB. And I sobbed all the way home putting countless drivers in untold peril as I accidentally missed my exit and headed toward Wisconsin. That wasn't part of my plan at all, My nest was FINALLY empty and here I was crying. Sheesh

After a good cry, I arrived home with a renewed energy. I planned a date night for my beloved Moondoggy and me right at home complete with a nice dinner and wine and no one to interrupt our complete sentences. So, imagine my surprise when Youngest walked in the door at 5 p.m. asking what was for dinner. Home from college on our first empty nest weekend? This was not part of my plan. What could I do? I set a place for him too and marveled at how mature he seemed after 1 month of college. His quick wit and biting sense of humor cracked us up all weekend. What a gift!

Luckily, Moondoggy and I secretly implemented a back-up plan last June that entailed building a house in the California desert And so, we really do have an empty nest. . . in California and we get to visit it every so often. At least that's OUR plan - for now. Because what I have been reminded of from all of this? I don't really make the plan at all.

CHAPTER TWELVE

CRUISING

I was 22 years old when I moved to small-town America. I had lived a host of other places; St. Louis, San Francisco, suburban Detroit. My point, in a word, - URBAN. So, being closer in age to the teenagers than I was to "grown ups," when I moved to this town, I was curious about what teens did in a small town for entertainment. I received this response, "Mostly, we cruise."

Really.

To me and anyone from the greater-Detroit area, cruising is an animal of a distinct species and it hasn't got anything to do with a boat (unless you are talking about a land Yacht.) Woodward Ave. is a multi-lane byway that runs from downtown Detroit to Pontiac in a 30-mile-loop and is bisected by roads aptly named by the mile they represent. A brilliant concept, enabling anyone to know how to get places. I often wonder why other cities haven't adopted this technique.

I lived at 16 mile. My husband lived on Woodward just beyond 17 mile. Eminem made a movie about 8 mile; the official boarder into Detroit (but I feel obligated to point out that HE lived in Warren - another suburb) and

Bob Seeger sings about it. Cruising Woodward is a famous pass time.

We, as teens, just as the teens before us and those since would cruise Woodward Ave for lack of anything better to do. I drove a butterscotch Dodge Magnum, a green Chrysler Newport. And when neither was available? A mustard-colored Triumph Spitfire. On a good night, we would stop at one of the party stores between 12 and 14 Mile (another Michigan phenomena - they are liquor stores that also sell chips, and sometimes other paraphernalia. . .so I heard) buy some beer and head toward Detroit. (Oh - stop clucking your tongue. The drinking age was 18. . .it wasn't hard to do. And, . . .it was the 70's.) We would not turn around until we had seen a hooker, a pimp or a junkie OR, the big score? witnessing a crime in progress. This all interspersed with drag racing, "burn outs" and trash talking out the windows. Ok, so we didn't really do that racing stuff but we did participate in a little mooning (you know, pressed ham?) My friend Susan was known down the "mile road" rows as the chick with fried eggs. What's a fried egg you ask? It's a full moon in the upper frontal quadrant of the body. I hate to tell you how many boyfriends she garnered through that action alone. . . or how long any of them lasted.

Last summer, I spent two nights cruising Woodward Ave in a 1967 Pontiac Grand Prix convertible along with (no lie) a million other classic cars. In what is touted as The Woodward Dream Cruise, this HUGE event attracts driving enthusiasts from all over the country. The sad part is, 95 percent of the guys cruising Woodward averaged 60 years of age on the low end. Cars creep along at two to three miles an hour and crowds of people line the side of the road screaming, "Lite 'em up!" encouraging these old guys to leave copious amounts of rubber on the road. And they do it. Even sadder? Mooning looks more like whales breaching and fried eggs like bovine udders. And if I see another mullet on a bald head, I might just gag. But, I do it year after year. Why?

Because that's what we do on Woodward Ave.

Chapter Thirteen

Can I Interest You in Some Property?

Have you ever received that dinner-hour or early evening phone call from an overly enthusiastic phone solicitor? What do you do? Listen and politely dismiss? Unload a mouthful of expletives or simply hang up? Well, that overly enthusiastic caller used to be me. Yeah, in high school, I was a phone solicitor for Lakes of the North, a resort community located just south of Gaylord, Michigan with headquarter offices located on the 30th floor of one of the first high rises in Southfield, MI. And, I can still recite the spiel including all answers to any objections given by the person on the other end - voice inflections and all. I was pretty good too. The idea was to schedule appointments (known in the biz as leads) with our representatives to come to their home and receive the free trip up north (code for sales pitch, of course) to see the beauty the Lakes of the North (LON) has to offer. Four leads a night equaled double pay, more leads in a night garnered even more bonuses. I once took home a two week paycheck in the amount of $872 for four hours work a night (20 hours a week). That was the night I waltzed into the house and announced to my parents that I was going to forgo the whole college scene and go to work full-time in the phone room. A proud moment for them, I'm sure.

The phone room consisted of a long room with study carrels lining each wall - at least 30 of them. Each carrel had a phone and several Bresser sheets - phone book pages of sorts that were categorized by streets. That way when we made an appointment we could call the next-door neighbor and say, "Do you know the Smith's next door? The rep will be at their house at 6:30 tomorrow, would 7 p.m. or 7:30 be better for you?" After the appointment was made, we called over our manager to confirm the appointment. There were supposed to be bells at each station but we all just resorted to covering the mouthpiece of the phone shouting, "DING!" instead. There were a good 30 girls working there on any given day from many of the surrounding areas.

I had my 30th high school reunion last fall and spent some time with Maureen, who also worked the phone room (and if I was good - Mo was GREAT) which conjured up some long-forgotten images and deep belly laughs associated with LON. We had two managers, Val and Lorain who were also best friends. I can't begin to tell you how old Val was. She could have been 30 she could have been 50. Val probably stood 5' 2" but always wore Candiesmwith heels that put her around 5'7". She had very delicate features but the biggest, darkest Marlo Thomas "That Girl" head of hair you have ever seen. Texas-sized hair. She also wore thick black mascara that pulled her lashes up to her eye brows and reminded me of a cartoon cow's long eyelashes. Val chain smoked cigarettes often allowing her ash to grow to lengths long enough to curve before finally falling off as she tottered on her Candies from phone cubby to phone cubby. The bet was always where the next ash would fall. The outside was in direct opposition to her inside. Val was almost like a Den Mother with to girls . . .only in tight clothing. If you needed something, Val was there.   If I were to run into her today, I would expect her to look exactly the same.

Lorain was a Val wannabe. Lorain was in her 20's and wanted nothing more than to be a kept woman by one of the successful salesmen. Lorain had wild curly dark hair, constantly manicured and polished nails and a voice that like Fran Drescher only an octave higher. Lorain chain smoked too and spent a lot of time at the front of the room twirling her curly hair or pulling apart split ends just waiting for one of the salesmen to come in and flirt with her. While not as petite as Val, Lorain often traded clothes with her making her look more like a stuffed sausage with lip stick than another version of Val. She was not unattractive but, she had to work at looking good a little harder than Val.

I often wonder what happened to Val and Lorain. Lakes of the North still exists and I wouldn't be surprised if they were still there doing the same thing. Considering that, I'm glad my parents didn't allow that glorious $872 paycheck guide my future decisions because I'd hate to think of myself wearing 5" Candies, false eyelashes and smoking a cigarette without ever tapping off the ash or worse pulling apart my split ends waiting for a salesman to ask me out.

And by the way? We welcomed the yellers because what you don't know is this: We could put them on speaker so that the entire phone room could share in the laugh. And yes, we saved the best conversations for the office Christmas party.

CHAPTER FOURTEEN

LAST DANCE WITH MARY JANE

I am 48 years old. It's not a secret and I am not ashamed. I wear my age with a certain amount of confidence because it's really true: when you get older you care less and less what anyone thinks about you. I'm not ready for a purple dress and red hat yet - not because I wouldn't look good, but because I have an ongoing battle with my 17-year-old self and she wouldn't allow we to be caught dead in a purple dress.

Seventeen-year-old me and 48-year-old me make a unique duo. She follows me around like a shadow, slightly distorted and exaggerated but me none the less. And like most teenagers, she can be annoying - especially when she is right.

I see a lot of interesting things discarded on the side of the road when I am on a morning trek. I've seen the usual, abandoned underwear, half-empty bottles of booze and even money, but nothing compares to what I found the other day and how I handled it because 17-year-old me and 48-year-old me had vastly differing opinions.

I was walking down Second Street in front of the nursing home, deep in thought, when I made an extra step to avoid a plastic bag that looked, quite honestly, like pet

poo that someone dumped. It took about 20 more steps
before 17-year-old me grabbed my 48-year-old arm,
spun me around and directed back to the plastic bag.

48: What are you doing?
17: (Pointing to the baggie) Look! Pick it up!
48: I'm not touching that thing, I don't even know what
it is. You pick it up.
17: (somewhat disgusted with my reaction) It's a bag
of pot.
48: Marijuana? How do YOU know?
17: Are you serious? I am 17-year-old you. It's the
70's.
48: What should I do with it? Maybe it belongs to
someone.
17: (Looks around) Yeah - from the nursing home? Get
real.
48: Let's just keep walking.
17: You are going to just ignore a perfectly good bag of
pot - what's wrong with you?
48: What am I going to do with it?
17: (assessing and thinking) You could sell it.
48: To who? The Cancer Center? . . .You think it's a
dime bag or a nickel?
17: (Pointing at me) Ah ha! You do remember!

So I bowed to 17-year-old me, stooped to pick up the
bag and smell it because, I still wasn't convinced it
wasn't dog poop. As I opened the baggie and took a
sniff, who should come tooling down the street but a
local police officer stopping to say, "Hey."

17: Cops! RUN!!!!!!!!!!

48: (Holding 17 firmly in my grip) You are not running anywhere. I am in charge here so sit yourself down missy and wait until I am finished.

After a quick exchange of small town greetings with the officer, I showed him the bag I had just found sitting on the curb and not just because he had witnessed me giving it the sniff test and I wanted to exonerate myself. He donned a pair of latex gloves, opened the bag and verified that yes, it was a bag of marijuana. Placing the bag in the trunk of the cruiser he took out his notebook to make a report.

Cop: Do you want your name mentioned?

17: NOOOOOOOOO!

48: It's going in the paper, right?

Cop: It will be in the next edition.

48: (Thinking about the implications) No - just stick with , "anonymous."

17: (Looking me directly in the eye) Thank you!

Cop: (Smiling) I hear ya.

And, I think somewhere his 17-year-old self was asking, "How much do you want for it?"

Chapter Fifteen

But The Possibilities Are Endless

Oh My Gosh! I've gone and done it. There is no turning back and no opportunity for denial. I took the first steps into a new realm of existence.   I have become a bag lady. No, no, I don't carry bags full of bric a brac or push a grocery cart. Heavens no. I don't talk to myself (or at least I don't do it out loud) and I don't scare other people (unless I am feeling snarky and haven't had my roots dyed in awhile and there's a cranky, mouthy kid in a store, I might give him the old stink eye and watch him cower in fear with a certain amount of glee.) But, I have to ask myself what in the world possessed me to take someone else's trash?

I was on one of my morning walks, in fact it was goal-oriented in fashion – I was walking from the lowest point in town (the River) to the highest point (top of Hill road) which takes me through town, past the new Middle School and through Northern Heights subdivision. It was also trash day. I was walking along minding my own business, solving the problems of the world when there in front of me were not one but TWO wooden chairs. Really they were just sitting there right next to the trash cans waiting to be scooped up and crushed by the powerful truck. I was compelled to rescue them.

This launched a firestorm of conversation in my head that began with, "Don't be stupid – we don't need any more chairs," whizzed right through, "My God, they are like a huge canvas," and ended with "Finish your walk and if they are there on the way back, then you can think about them." I remained true to my walk, summiting the top of Hill Road and retracing my steps back home . . . back by the trash in Northern Heights.

Sadly, it was clear that the behemoth truck that devours trash had been by in my absence. Resigned, I ambled down the road when I swear the sun rays peaked out from the clouds long enough to shine on. . .yes, yes. . .my chairs still sitting there next to the now empty trash can. I mustered up my courage as I got closer to the house because I am NOT your run-of-the-mill trash picker, hell no. I marched up to the door and rang the bell alarming the really big, really loud barking Rottweiler who jumped at the door until the owner opened it and I asked for permission. Yes, I did. I out right asked if they intended to toss those PERFECTLY GOOD wood chairs out with their rubbish and would they mind if I came back with my car and picked them up? The guy seemed quite disgusted but said, "Have at 'em lady," and slammed the door before the Rottweiler lunged through the screen and ate my little dog for a snack. I was so happy I skipped, yes SKIPPED back home, got in the car and hauled those beauties back to my house promptly trying to hide them before any of the males at my house discovered my bounty.

It took all of 15 minutes before Oldest Son noticed the chairs, texted his brother and his father and I was busted. Moondoggy thinks it's funny now to slowly drive by houses where large broken items are sitting out with the trash and ask me if I feel like shopping. He even refers to Trash Day as Shopping Day. Ha. Ha. Just wait until he sees what I make out of these! In the meantime, if you think you might be throwing out something I might like, just call my cell phone direct – it will be much easier on all of us.

CHAPTER SIXTEEN

AN OUNCE OF PREVENTION

Healthcare. There, I said it and now I'll stand back while the people from both sides of the issue line up baring teeth and waving baseball bats. It is, absolutely, a political hot button that conjures up the most biting words with the teeth marks often showing up on the best of friends. I am concerned about the Healthcare Crisis too, but my reasons are a little different and some may seem a wee bit selfish, but I have a solution and it is nothing short of genius.

I'm all about preventative care. It only makes sense, doesn't it, to avoid a disease instead of waiting for it to extend it's clammy hands around your neck and then worry about the costly treatment? My own genetics point to heart related issues. I'm not happy about this but the die has been cast and the best thing I can do is try to live my life in a preventative manner which, to me, means taking steps to avoid heart disease. And I think insurance should be *more* than happy to pay for it.

This is my proposal: I think insurance should pay for a lifetime of red wine. Simple right? Everyone knows that the tannins of the grape skin found in red wine have been found to be beneficial to the heart. In fact, a glass of wine a day is a RECOMMENDATION for optimum heart health. I'd say that's a no brainer. In fact, if I were the insurance companies, I would be making tracks to my local winery to make a sweet deal whereby they partner with the vintner to have cases of red wine sent to their clients every month. Then they could partner with UPS or even FedEx and get an even sweeter deal just by volume alone and I think that is tax deductible for them, so win, win, win.

And here's how it would go: At any reasonable age after turning the age of majority. . . .say 21, a required medical check-up would be required. After a complete health history, physical work-up, blood panel and a Heart Score test, the freshly minted 21-year-old would begin a lifelong preventative program that begins with a required glass of wine every day.

The beauty of wine is that it keeps. So, it would be highly cost effective for insurance companies to send it out by the case on a monthly basis. I'm thinking two cases a month would be appropriate. In fact, why not vary the reds every month? Merlot. Chianti. Burgundy. The scope of this is huge. Wineries would be in competition with each other over insurance company contracts, and, no doubt producing in larger quantities. . .which would require more workers. A boon to the economy really. On the plus side, for the average guy is a fully stocked wine bar. . .which would require all sorts of wine accessories. Wine cooler. Aerator. Cork screws. Glasses. I can just feel the economy strengthening as I get healthier.

Forget medicinal marijuana - that's small potatoes , I think red wine should be categorized as heart medicine and thus, required by law to be provided by and paid for by our health insurance companies. An ounce of prevention is worth a pound of cure? I say four ounces and make it a fine red. Now to figure out a way to add dark chocolate into the equation.

Chapter Seventeen

When Halloween Goes Global

My sister called the other day to share her latest assessment of life, as we do with each other from time to, when she stumbled upon a subject so glorious I just could not let it go. And because it would be poor form to not give credit to the genius who conceived this gem, I have to give a shout out to my sister's highly revered hairdresser – Tammy.

There was this costume party coming up and a group of women were discussing what to wear when Tammy suggested they all dress as GIRL SCOUTS! Not just any girl scout mind you, but as COUGAR GIRL SCOUTS! They would all wear their uniforms with enough cleavage and bra showing to have no mistaking the intent. They would wear a sash that contained different levels of achievement badges (the "Walk of Shame" badge, the "Triple Play" badge and, of course, "Proper Condom Application" badge) and carry canteens filled with cosmopolitans. Their troop number? 69!

When I heard this, I howled. But, I could not just enjoy the laugh for the moment because the scope of this is priceless. Let's drop the "girl" part, because face it, none of us look 10 anymore. Let's call ourselves Cougar Scouts. And let's forgo the traditional scout uniform and get a little creative. I myself have always coveted the white patent leather go-go boots from the early '70's so I think they should be the official footwear. I also like a cute tennis skirt with built in panties, after all, we may be cougar's but we are not easy so it will take some fancy talking to get to the goodies. Any color is acceptable but it must be paired with a black tank top. I mean we are hot – temperature hot that is, and we are NOT going to be burdened by unnecessary layering. Besides, black is thinning. To accessorize the ensemble, we need a belt – animal print of course, a matching wristlet to carry lipstick, compact and cab fare. Good scouts do carry canteens and they should be filled at all times with the beverage of choice (mine is red wine) and instead of binoculars, I suggest blinged-out cheater glasses. If you really want to carry something more binocularly, how about a View Master with a picture wheel of gorgeous men? Brownies wore beanies, Girl Scouts wore berets, Cougar Scouts will wear a scarf as a headband (with or without a Hollywood Bump It and fake hair) and, of course, a tiara for formal meetings. Meetings will be established by each troop with an annual meeting in either Florida or California on alternate years with an optional spa visit mid year. We could sing altered camp song's:

Do your boobs hang low, do they wobbled too and fro

Can you tie 'em in a knot, can you tie 'em in a bow
Can you throw 'em over your shoulder like a continental
soldier
Do your boobs hang low

Ok - now in rounds. . .

Forget Halloween, I see this as a national club with
troops not only in every state, but every town across the
U.S. This could be huge! But what about troop dues, you
ask? Hell, there are no dues – we've already paid 'em!

Chapter Eighteen

The Fine Art of Speaking Female

I've written about it before; this bizarre world of the XY chromosome. I pride myself on taking note of the differences - often. It never dawned on me though, that in my day-in-day-out living in this XY environment I had somehow become numb to the side effects. In fact, I had become so numb to Malespeak that I ACCEPTED compliments uttered in said language without considering the lack of expression or sincerity. I hang my head in shame at this admission.

It was the dawn of a new year and with that came my annual, "I hate my hair" tantrum and the usual phone call to the salon begging for the first available appointment. Lucky for me, they had a space for me in less than two hours - not enough time to change my mind.

So, I skipped off to the salon and uttered the words every hairdresser dreams of, "Cut it off." And, lo upon finally looking at myself in the mirror, I found I liked it. It was, well. . . perky. Short, but not too short. Longer in the front, bobbed in the back. It was bouncin' and behavin' and I practically danced out of the salon with that, "feel like a woman," feeling soon after arriving for a face-to-face with my youngest son. My males don't speak Female at all so when Youngest asked, "Where were you?" I actually had to point to my head and say, "Hairdresser?" His response? "Oh." Not only does he not speak or understand Female, I think he lumps it in with security lanyards at school and daylight savings time under, "That's stupid."

Moondoggy, after 33 years with me at least pays lip service to Femalespeak, albeit in a monotone inflection. So, when he walked in the door, he immediately noted that a change had occurred and with but the slightest scrutiny said, "You got your hair cut. It looks nice." It. Looks. Nice. I had just been bestowed with the greatest of his Femalespeak efforts and I didn't expect much more. I didn't know that MORE was even a realistic possibility. That is. . .until New Year's Eve when we went to our Danish friends' house for a party and I stumbled on the little known fact that some men DO speak Female and I have been gypped for the last 33 years.

The Erstwhile Earth Mother Kim and her wise husband Jens The Great Dane (Pronounced "Yens" - he's Danish and he'll play that card if he needs to) have four daughters (whose names all begin with "K" - it's very Danish) between 16 and 22 years old. For Jens, meant he had to suffer through four separate female puberties in four separate phases in a six-year time frame. He also had to comfort countless broken hearts, buy mass quantities of feminine products on a moment's notice without embarrassment and juggle five cases of PMS at any given time of the month. Ergo he naturally acquired the fine art of Femalespeak. This is how the conversation went down:

Doorbell rings and The Great Dane greets us at the door - me with a big hug and Moondoggy with a "guy" handshake. And then he steps back from me and LOOKS ME DIRECTLY IN THE EYE and says, "I LOVE your hairstyle!" But it doesn't stop there; oh no he follows with THIS, "It makes you look so much younger and thinner." And then he finishes with a, "Wow!"

I positively BLUSHED. And I admit it; I am a sucker for cheesy compliments when they are delivered in any manner that doesn't sound like a canned comment (i.e. if I said you had a beautiful body would you hold it against me? Yeah, only during a choke hold buddy.) I turned to Moondoggy and said, "Jens knows how to speak Female!" Which, I think, must have fallen on Moondoggy's "Spouse" ear (the one that never listens to what I say) because I mentioned it again the next morning. I said, "You could take some lessons from Jens on how to speak Female." And Moondoggy, looking at me like I had grown another head, replied, "I thought Jens spoke Danish."

Chapter Nineteen

One Word is Worth a Thousand Meanings

The English language is one of the most difficult languages for anyone not raised speaking the language to fully comprehend. What with words that are spelled the same, pronounced the same yet have vastly different meanings. . .words like, well "Like," it's a wonder we can understand each other at all. I can like (as in enjoy) something (Facebook encourages me to like lots of things) or something can be like. . .as in math: Are the amounts like? We've all seen the homonyms like (meaning, "as in") read and read. Or lie and lie. However, it has been my experience that perhaps the complicated meaning surrounding the simplest words is more of a problem for the average American - specifically the average American male. . .with the name Moondoggy.

I learned early in my marriage that the male of the my particular family species tend toward the extremely literal when they speak and are not capable of stepping back to see the deeper meaning of even simple words unless prodded and, yes sometimes even shamed. It's not a fault exactly, it's more like (meaning, "comparable to") a handicap. The sad part is that they don't seem to understand WHY the entire population of females in their lives think it's a problem. Pity. Take, for example, the word LOOK.

My sister-in-law, who likes to be thought of as Queen of the Universe (and we allow her that moniker only because she can dispense professional medical advice to us for free) lost her beloved Portuguese Water Dog, Kelsey, last summer after a long and love-filled life. My brother-in-law, her husband, would rather chew broken glass than to have a pet but tolerated having a dog all of those years for his daughters. Tolerated. Rarely did he refer to Kelsey as anything more than, "dog" and "it." The truth is, he believes the best pets are ceramic (an opinion held by my own Moondoggy as well.). So, when Kelsey died, in deference to his heartbroken women, my brother-in-law didn't say much and reserved his "Happy Dance" for private moments in his man cave.

Several weeks after Kelsey was gone, Queen of the Universe announced that she was going to look at Golden-doodle puppies. Brother-in-law grunted but didn't say much. Queen made this trek to "look" at the puppies four times. FOUR TIMES! When she announced that she had, in fact, fallen in love with a puppy and made a deposit - Brother-in-law's head spun around three times and he spat," I thought you were only going to LOOK!" Now I ask you, if you are looking, (meaning, "observing") at your better half going to look (meaning, "bond") at something four times, do you think she

WON'T eventually come home with a something? How many times did he "look" at a 2009 Corvette before ordering one and do you think for one moment that the Queen of the Universe thought he was "just looking" without the intent to purchase?

So it should come as no shock that I witnessed the following story unfold at the annual family Christmas last weekend.

My sainted, cat-loving other sister-in-law had just recovered from a fairly traumatic fall fraught with invasive surgeries, obstructions, nose tubes and other horrors not for the faint of heart. And stoically, she made it through. Sainted Sister-in-Law did all of this without the comfort of her two beloved cats who had both passed on to the great scratching post in the sky within the past two years. Now, my other brother-in-law, is not a fan of cats, but had been a good sport with Sainted Sister-in-Law's cats. After all, Sainted Sister-in-Law and the cats were a package deal. As her recovery progressed, Sainted Sister found herself yearning to get out and about. Other Brother-in-Law suggested it might cheer Sainted Sister up if she were to go to the SPCA and look at cats. She thought that was both thoughtful and sensitive of Other Brother (and, I might add, worth several hundred valuable Husband Points redeemable at moments of poor judgment) and took him up on the suggestion.

Over dinner that evening, an excited and re-energized Sainted Sister informed Other Brother that she had found three cats and one dog that she connected with and even asked if he would care to go back and help her select a pet. Other Brother's eyes bulged out of his head meeting the lenses of his glasses and he spat, "I thought you were just going to LOOK, *not* bring one home!"

Can you imagine? I mean really, why not just offer a chocoholic a Godiva and then take it away, risking certain maiming? I am pretty sure that when Other Brother decided to look at SLR cameras, Sainted Sister knew it meant he was going to BUY one (which he did - a really expensive one!)

Funny thing about the simple words like (meaning, "for example") Look-- you can take them at face value or you just might find yourself looking (meaning, "eating your words") into the furry face of a brand new family member and it might be a smart move to like (meaning, "pretend to be thrilled by") it.

Chapter Twenty

Step by Step

That great social networking tool known as Facebook has caught on wildly with increasingly older members. I believe this is typical of everything in our society really. Take fashion: What has been in fashion for the younger set takes a good three years to catch up to people my age (which explains my recent purchase of a pair of skinny jeans and UGG boots) and we wear it timidly at first then,with the first positive feedback begin wearing the style as if we OWN it. The same thing has happened with Facebook much to the disgust of my youngest child. He thinks I am addicted to Facebook when actually, I am simply unemployed = FB LOL :)

I spent the better part of the morning on the phone with my folks yesterday getting them set up on Facebook so that they too can view the activity of their grandkids, nieces, etc.

Shoot. Me. Now.

Thankfully, I was on the phone with my step mom who is much easier to communicate with than my dad. Had it been my dad on the phone this is how I believe the conversation would have gone. . .

Dad: Hello Judi!

Me: Hey Dad, what's up?

Dad: Say, we are trying to buy a Facebook here but don't know where to find the software.

Me: There is no software Dad, just go to the website and it will walk you through the process.

Dad: How does it work without software?

Me: (forcing a smile) Just go to your address bar and type in w-w-w dot Facebook dot com.

Dad: The http thing disappeared, how do I get it back?

Me: (grimacing) Just type in w-w-w dot Facebook dot com.

Dad: Ok it's not doing anything.

Me: Try hitting "enter" Dad.

Dad: Oh, ok it wants me to set up an account. I'm NOT going to pay for this am I?

Me: No, it's free.

Dad: Because I am not going to give out my personal information here. Anyone could get this and send it all over the internet!

Me: They call it an account, but there is no money exchange. You don't have to give them any information.

Dad: Oh yeah? Well, why do they want to know what high school I went to. That seems suspect!

Me: (head in hands) Never mind Dad. This isn't going to work.

Dad: Why not?

Me: Because you need to go buy the correct software first.

That should keep him busy for awhile.

Chapter Twenty One

I'll Have What She's Having

Recently, one of the athletic shoe companies asked women to find their inner athlete. It got me to thinking. It had been awhile since Inner Athlete and I had gotten together and I was wondering how she was. So, I set out to find her. That is to say, I searched for my Inner Athlete in all the usual spots with no luck. When I found her she was at the beach sitting in a comfy chair by the water sipping a boat drink wondering why I was dressed in t-shirt, sweats and running shoes.

There was a time when we were one. It's no secret that I lack the ability to execute keen sport skills that entail any sort of teamwork and, well, skill. Too much thinking and strategizing while breathing hard. . .not my style. But, I have been involved in sports that don't have others depending on me for a win.

I was raised in Michigan where skiing and skating are winter requirements. We even had a rink in our backyard where I could practice my arabesques and spins to my heart's content until the neighborhood kids wanted to play hockey. I even participated in the hockey until I realized I don't like getting my head cracked on ice. And after seeing home movies of my little 10-year-old self skating, pathetically raising one leg behind me to a height of, oh two inches, I realized the hysterical laughing I was hearing was my Inner Athlete rolling on the floor holding her stomach and howling, "Oh my - we really thought we could skate!" Bahahahahahah!

In the late '90s and early 2000s I was into kickboxing. And I really did love that. Nothing beats a workout where you kick and pummel the absolute living hell out of a bag while imagining the face of your choice. That is, until you kick hard enough to loosen a bone fragment in your right knee, requiring surgery and the discovery of massive arthritis. My inner athlete packed her gear and left on vacation.

Another surgery later, this time a lovely and time-consuming achilles reattachment and bone excision, I realized my inner athlete was on to something. One last time, I clicked into my skis and went to tackle a run with friend Tammy whose inner athlete is beautifully meshed with her inner child and wise adult (some people are lucky that way.) And guess what? I had an epiphany. I don't enjoy skiing anymore. I'm not sure I ever did. My feet ache, my knees throb, and really? My form is horrendous. I could hear Inner Athlete clapping with joy.

I'm glad that I was encouraged to find my Inner Athlete. I like the way she thinks. I am going to put the skis on Craig s List and buy myself a beach chair. Together, my inner athlete and I will walk the beach, swim the ocean (or pool) and enjoy exercise on our own terms. Shape skis anyone????

Chapter Twenty two

Not By The Hair On My Chinny Chin Chin

I just got a new pair of bifocals. Not the fancy schmancy progressive no line jobs though. I've had them and can safely say that I despise them probably as much as I despise Las Vegas. I know, I know I defaulted back to the archaic and that's ok, it's worth it if I can see clearly from all angles instead of following my nose (that's what they tell you with "no lines.") Well, it was until I came face to face with, well, my face that I realized how I have been kidding myself for years.

It was, for lack of a better example, like reconciling with my naked body. I've developed an effective and efficient relationship with my large mirror when I step out of the shower. I am fortunate enough that I can reach my towel and dry off in the shower thereby allowing me to drape my body with the towel when I head out to my closet for clothing. With nothing more than a fleeting glance as I pass, the mirror and I both acknowledge that work needs to be done but there is no need to rub it in. Not so with the close-up make-up mirror while wearing new bifocals. That mirror just screamed "FOUL!" I think it suffers from little mirror syndrome but, whatever.

The view from my new bifocals was daunting. There are lines and crevices on my face. Who knew? Worse yet, there are traces of yesterdays mascara dotting areas below my eyes and there are HUGE ugly red veins IN my eyes. I really thought I had good friends - the kind that tell you about the chive or pepper speck in your tooth but apparently that courtesy stops at old, crusty make-up. I stopped worshipping the sun in the 80's and started wearing 30 sunblock at all times. . .but that hasn't stopped the sun inspired age spots that are appearing on my cheeks. The little "whiskers" that start to appear on the aging female chin (and admit it gals, we ALL feel them) - the ones that feel like spikes? Well, they really LOOK like huge spikes too. I try to pluck them but sometimes I just end up curling them instead. The way I see it, I have two choices here: I can continue to put on make-up without my glasses - a beauty filter of sorts; kinda like smearing vaseline on a camera lens or, I can gracefully accept these new discoveries on my face, embrace them, name them even (and what the heck, put a bow in the chin hair) and welcome them into my family.

Think I'll go with the former!

CHAPTER TWENTY THREE

I LIKE ME AN XX FLICK

The preponderance of the Y chromosome in my immediate family makes it almost impossible for me to win the movie battle. If it isn't filled with high speed chases in cool cars, or following a spy throughout the eastern block during the cold war or littered with "quality" kills – I generally don't get to see it. I feel justified in this complaint. The last movie I got to choose from the video store was, "Marley and Me," and I know it was male approved because of Jennifer Aniston. I can tell you the last "chic flick" Moondoggy and I saw at the theater was "Mama Mia" and I'm still paying for that one. There, that's it.

Tonight, I saw, "Julie and Julia" in the theater. On my own. Along with six other women, four of whom were having a girls night, two were mother and daughter and then there was me. The prospect of going to a movie by myself isn't as daunting as the fear that I may be the only one in the theater and that is positively creepy. But there I was until a few minutes before the film began sitting in a theater all by my lonesome fighting the urge to leave because I was bound and determined to see a movie that *I* wanted to see.

Meryl Streep as Julia Child was utterly delightful (her performance inspires me to start speaking like Julia) while I was only mildly entertained by the character of Julie. Perhaps it is because she is admittedly self absorbed, or while living in a 900 sq. foot walk up in Queens, NY she could magically afford some of the exotic foods that Julia Child's book calls for. Or maybe it is the fact that after 365 days of following Julia's recipes, which make Paula Deen's butter fetish look like light cooking, she didn't gain any weight. I might even call her a bitch for that very reason alone but I think the real reason I had issues with the whole Julie side of the story is this – Julie is a writer who starts blogging; writing daily insights and updates as she cooks her way through Julia Child's book. That's it! THAT'S IT???? One year later, she is offered several book deals; even a movie deal. Hmph. Did I mention it is a true story? Ok, I'm not above a little jealousy every now and again.

However, I digress. Sitting in the theater with six other woman was freeing. It gave me full permission to laugh at Streep's goofiness, the interaction with her sister that only sisters can understand, and full on guffaw at the moments when Julie's mother tells her at one moment she can't follow through and then chastising her in the next for following through to the exclusion of everything else. It allowed me to understand the French language without having to translate for someone else causing me to lose my place in the scene. It allowed me to enjoy a full 2 hours all by myself without concern for anyone else. I'm not used to that, but I really, REALLY like it.

Blogging 365 days with Julia Child? Why didn't I think of that? Oh, and FYI? Sometimes the Y chromosome is superfluous!

Chapter Twenty Four

When a Man Loves a Woman

I know you remember it so don't even pretend you don't. THE movie. Yes, THAT one where the school starts prepping you days beforehand and whether you are a boy or girl determines what you see, where you see it and with whom. I'm a girl. I got to watch the epic of my womanhood in the library with all of the other girls in fifth grade along with their mothers. Did I honestly learn anything from the animated version of my uterus and ovaries other than if you look at the plumbing from a cartoon point of view, the whole thing kind of resembles a cartoon cow head (see fig. 1) ?

Nope.

fig. 1   The Female Uterus, Fallopian
                    Tubes and Ovaries

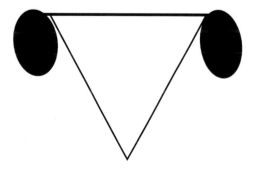

The school nurse who presented my program - dressed in her nursey whites I might add, did so with clinical terminology and crisp, clipped speech. Lovely. I couldn't freakin' wait for my big day. . . except that my big day had already arrived about three months before THE movie so I knew the whole thing was a lie. My mother already knew I wasn't buying into that delusion! And let me tell you, in an era just prior to pads that use adhesive, where the appliances for the newly womanized included bulky pads with long tails that attached to a belt (more like a harness really, but not as delicate a word) meant to be worn under the clothing, I saw no beauty in the situation. I did not feel like I had emerged into a new era of womanhood, instead I felt like I was thrown into a alternate world where all females were forced to walk bowlegged to accommodate for the unwieldy pad between their legs and pretending that no one could possibly notice. In short, it was Hell. We walked out of THE movie with a fistful of pamphlets that I was directed to read and learn more as well as a coupon for my "very first" Kimberly Clark product. Thanks loads.

Well, God was surely smiling on me the day I conceived my children because He decided that the pesky Y chromosome would supersede and I procreated two males thereby circumventing the lie I might have had to perpetuate on my own children had they been girls. I would have no "beautiful" womanhood moment to guide a daughter through, no cramps to alleviate, no PMS to shield myself from. I lucked out and I decided early on to take advantage of the situation when the time arrived. And luckily, BFF Cindy who grew up in a family of females and shared my desire for fun was right by my side when we started prepping our boys for THE movie.

Society being what it is, some things have changed. The most glaring change for me was that THE movie is shown during a period of Health class during the day so no uncomfortable special "night meeting." The other interesting change is that while parents are encouraged to preview the film, they are not encouraged to attend the session itself. Finally, while I got some perfume smelling brochures and a coupon for my troubles, these days kids get a full swag bag of goodies to keep complete with deodorant and soap for the boys and a complete array of feminine products for the girls.

The day before the big film debut, I sat my oldest son down and attempted to lay the groundwork. I told him, "No offense, but they will tell you that you are starting to stink and that deodorant would be an ideal solution (along with daily bathing and clean clothes.) They are also going to tell you about the changes that will start happening in your body and what to expect. Would you like me to tell you about that?" He responded with an emphatic, "NO,' followed by, "Can I go now?" Before he ran out the door, I finished with this:

"Hey! I have a great idea! Maybe Cindy, who is a nurse after all, and I should come to the movie too? You know, we could be there for you guys if you have any

questions or if anyone else in the class has questions. What do you think?"

Before he could verbalize the horror that appeared across his face, I added:

"I could pop some popcorn, just like at the theater, and bring it in. We can scoop it up in Dixie cups and share it with the class. I'll bet everyone would like that."

He didn't fully hear the last sentence or two because by then he had barreled out the door and headed next door to BFF Cindy's where I am sure he met up with her son heading out the door to our house with the same abject fear. I tried not to snicker too loud.

The morning of the day of THE movie, as the boy was heading down to the bus stop, I kissed him goodbye and as he ran to the I street called out, "Hey! What time should I be there today?" Can you believe the kid pretended like he didn't even hear me???!!

He never mentioned how the day went or whether he was ever in fear that I might show up to "help", but I did find the contents of his swag bag neatly arranged on his dresser the next morning so perhaps he got more out of the whole thing than I ever did.

CHAPTER TWENTY FIVE

WHAT A MAN WON'T DO FOR. . .

WARNING: *If you are my parent or my child or a family member of any kind, this is fair and serious warning to NOT read the following entry. If you choose to ignore this admonishment then I WILL NOT be responsible for your disturbing nightmares or any therapy bills you may incur. Don't say I didn't warn you.*

I started knitting again after a several-year break. And, because I find myself incapable of reading knitting patterns and instructions (seriously, do you know what K2tog, SST, MK1 and continue round means????), I had to enlist the help of a friend. So, one snowy afternoon when she was not seeing patients, I sat in the living room of my friend and veteran knitter Erstwhile Earthmother Kim. With her guidance, I learned how to cast on and knit using four double-pointed needles. These are NOT big long needles but more of a delicate thin metal needle about 5" long requiring nimble dexterity and strong cheater glasses. But, I did it.

I went home and in the course of a week knitted two pairs of mittens and a hat and was starting on a pair of socks, but that isn't really what this story is about. You see, during the beginning stages of the socks, I realized I had to stop and let the dog out before heading to an appointment when the phone rang. And that final event, the phone ringing threw my normally controlled mind into overload.

Several hours later I returned to the knitting only to realize that my fourth needle was missing. I looked under the yarn pile, I looked under the ottoman, under the cushions, on the floor, under the rug. No needle. It had simply vanished which confounded me because I had all four needles when I set the project down. I was perplexed and knew it was time the to pull out the big guns.

When Moondoggy walked in the door that evening I told him about the missing needle and made him the queen of all offers. You know what I'm talking about ladies. If he could find the needle, I would bestow upon him what every husband desires and generally no longer receives from hardworking wives. He smirked and went off to change clothes. I figured he didn't believe me but in short order, I heard cushions being thrown off furniture, the couch being dragged into the middle of his room and when I went in to see what the ruckus was, I found him stuffing his arms DOWN into the bowels of the couch and chair in search of the missing knitting needle. I gasped and startled Moondoggy to attention. Breathing hard, he looked pointedly at me and declared, "I AM going to find that needle."

I left Moondoggy to his search already knowing that he wasn't going to find it there but allowing him to believe the possibility existed because hey - guys can dream too, right? If he thought there was a chance of THE reward, he was happy.

After dinner, I sympathetically suggested that perhaps he may find it somewhere else, made it sound almost like I was *begging* to give him said reward. He continued the search in every other part of the house and, quite frankly, I was wondering where in the world that needle could have gone to myself. I decided to pop some popcorn and give up for the night.

As I chomped on my version of nirvana (low fat popcorn sprayed with butter flavored Pam), I dropped a kernel that landed squarely in my cleavage. I pulled the neckline out to fish out the corn when what do you think I found tucked between the girls? Yes, that double pointed needle somehow must have found it's way down the front of my top and into my bra earlier in the day and, somehow worked it's way into a position where I could not feel it! Well, I just burst out laughing all over when I found it and then slowly pulled it out to show Moondoggy whose lower lip puffed out in the most pathetic yet carefully crafted boo boo lip I have ever seen. "NO!" said I firmly-- after all he didn't find it, I did.

Last night Moondoggy came home from work and kissed me, placing his hands squarely on the girls. I stepped back and asked him, "What are you doing?"
"Just checking for knitting needles."

Chapter Twenty Six

One Man's Eagle is Another Man's Bird

Last weekend we drove up to Wausau, Wisconsin with a large group of people for our annual ski weekend. We always check into the hotel as a Ski Club when the truth is, most are really snowboarders and we aren't really a club-- but it's a good time and the group looks forward to it every year. We set off at 7 a.m. and stopped to pick up my son's friend who was riding with us. As we got underway, my youngest quietly leans over to friend and says, "So you know my mom is going to point out wildlife all the way up." Never mind that I have known the friend all of his life and we have taken him on long driving vacations before and they are both 19 years old, my son imparts this wisdom as if we had never met. I scoffed. I have lived in northern Illinois for 27 years and am quite non-plussed by deer in the yard, raccoons under the house and the like. But, as I was noting this to the snarky teens, a Bald Eagle soared just 10 feet above the car and, well, like a shiny object, it caught my attention. Yes, I pointed it out. I might have squealed with delight. Who wouldn't? Apparently, our children. Somewhere between 1969 and 2010 the Bald Eagle, the regal bird that came dangerously close to extinction, our national symbol of freedom, was relegated to the status just another big bird. I should have seen this coming.

Ten years ago I did a stint teaching outdoor education to kids who came to the camp mostly from Chicago schools. I taught Team Building challenges, Ravine Study, Owl Pellet Dissection and Ethics in Nature. This last session entailed breaking kids into small groups, giving them a scenario with three possible outcomes with only one being the "ethical" choice, and having the group come to a conclusion and explain the rationale. So, I had this group from some she she poo poo prep school in Chicago where the girls were freaked out by moths and mosquitoes and the boys didn't want to get dirt on their shoes. We broke up into groups and I gave them their scenario:

You have found the perfect location to build your dream home. Before you begin to dig, it is discovered that there is a pair of nesting eagles right on the spot you want to build. Do you:

a) Cut the tree down and build anyway.
b) Sell the property to someone else and let them deal with it.
c) Move to a different location somewhere on the property.

This group of girls deliberated for quite a while, sometimes,whispering, sometimes raising their voices as they came to what they felt was their ethical decision.

When they finished, I asked them to present their scenario and their answer. I was greatly relieved and thrilled when they chose option "C" and asked why they had made that decision. The tallest of the three stepped forward and put her hand on her hip, "Well," she said as she threw her hair back, " If we cut the tree down, then we might not have any shade at all. And if we sold the property to someone else we would feel bad that they'd have to deal with those big birds squawking day and night so we figured the best thing to do was to go somewhere else on the property and hope the eagles eventually fly away."

What could I say? I congratulated them on their great job of reasoning and tucked the story away in my head. Living along a large river has enabled me to watch as the population of Bald Eagles has gained strength. There is a nest across from Ashelford Cove on the other side of the river that has been home to a pair of Bald Eagles for several years. I am still mesmerized by their majesty when they fly, breathless when I realize one is sitting quietly in a tree just above me and dying to share that thrill with anyone who will listen. Guess I have to scratch my kids off of that list. I'd hate to bore them with a big bird.

Chapter Twenty Seven

Well This Explains a Lot!

Google my father's name and several pages regarding his long career as Chief Patent Counsel with Chrysler Corp. pop up as well as his presidency of the AIPLA and his awards and associations with the College of Engineering at the University of Illinois. But keep looking and at the bottom of page two is a site called Extra that wrote a snippet about a performance my father gave in Danville, IL where he presented his rendition of the Andrews Sisters. . .all three of them. . .at once. Now that's the man everyone should know.

My father, was raised in Danville with the likes of Dick and Jerry Van Dyke, and more recently discovered, Andre Agassi's mother, Betty Dudley. My dad was the son of a teacher and basketball coach and a mother who would prefer a cute pair of strappy heels over house slippers any day of the week. My grandmother was a hottie but that's another story. My dad is the youngest of two, ergo, he learned the shortcuts of life from his brother. This happened early on when he discovered that it was just easier to roll from location to location than to bother learning to walk which garnered a marked number of snickers from those around him. He learned that he could elicit laughter fairly easily and thus became, for lack of a better word, a whore for the laugh. He still is.

The McCallum Theater in the Palm Springs area of California holds an annual amateur talent show. This "amateur" show, however, is much like a juried art show where the acts must submit tapes and after a rigorous elimination are "invited" to participate. A few years ago, dad sent in a tape. . .and made the cut. The amateur talent spent two weeks practicing, blocking and working with the professionals who emcee before their sell-out night. And so, with a good amount of pride and not a little fear, we flew out to see which of the "acts" could possibly have earned him a place in the California talent show. (Mind you, this is a man who once told me to tell my elementary art teacher that his greatest talent was that he drew flies.)

Now, you have to understand that my father has several "acts". In my lifetime the man has tried a number of personas including but not limited to banjo player (Jimmy Cracked Corn and none of us cared if we ever heard him play again), streaker (thank goodness he covered himself with a small towel), Abbott and Costello - a rendition of "Who's on First" where he played both Bud and Lou in a costume split in half so that one side angle was the baseball manager in a suit and the other was the baseball player in uniform. If you have ever seen the bit, you know it is a fast volley between two people that my father has condensed into one. He jumps from left profile to right with each line delivered leaving us all exhausted in the end. He has even gone so far as to cross dress for the laugh. My father has donned make-up, wig, skirt, camisole and knee highs in the interest of a good laugh. If any of the Andrews Sisters were to see him perform as THEM, they would run straight for the nearest plastic surgeon and demand an overhaul. Finally, he has his oldest and probably best, most professional bit pantomiming to a Spike Jones song. He started this act in high school and has perfected it to an unreal level. So, the question was. . . which of these acts did he submit?

The lights went down, a spotlight came up and out he walked on stage wearing a suit, a cockeye porkpie hat and carrying a coat hanger fashioned with string into a makeshift guitar. . .whew! Spike Jones it was and let me tell you, he KILLED (show biz lingo folks.) He was so good that when, during the middle of the "song" Spike Jones is singing he breaks out in laughter, the lady in front of me whispers to her husband, "He was doing such a nice job. . .why is he laughing???" I held my tongue in check because I wanted to tell her, "Because he is Lip Synching lady. . .it's all part of the bit," instead I just enjoyed the knowledge that my father does this so well that people believe he is actually performing the song live.

My dad has accomplished much in his life but I feel like his greatest victory is the ability to find the humor and go for the laugh after 75 years even when it makes the rest of us groan. He always believes it's worth a try. Now that is an accomplishment.

CHAPTER TWENTY EIGHT

IT'S NOT IN THE PARENT MANUAL

It's not often that I find myself at a loss for words, but that very thing occurred just the other day when I was in the process of writing about yet another job I worked where hi jinx eventually ensues. I was writing along at a pretty good clip feeling like I had the world by the tail when I stopped to look at my Facebook and my world tilted. No, it really wasn't a tilt, it was a full-on JOLT and it happened just like that. To be fair, there is no humor in what I have to offer.

I saw this post on Facebook and it stopped me cold. It said, "R.I.P Nick, you are in a better place." It only took a moment for me to confirm that Nick, a local boy who just turned 21 last week and celebrated with a trip down to the college he left for two years ago - Baylor University, had passed away; his battle with cancer finally over. Nick was two years younger then my oldest and two years older than my youngest. In a small town all of the kids know each other, but Nick ran with Youngest Son on the high school track team and I spent a good amount of voice power cheering for them both. Nick left for college an eager freshman but, it wasn't long before he was diagnosed with leukemia and he spent the next two years fighting, learning and loving life in spite of it all.

What I found completely heartbreaking was his final posted status on Facebook. He posted this the night before he passed:

The foreboding specter of spending most of the summer In a hospital getting sicker again is one I have neither the strength to overcome or that special someone to make the choice easier."

I am a trained hospice volunteer. I have spent countless hours with dying patients and I have experienced the gift that the dying have to offer. Even with the prophetic post, I didn't see this coming and when I found out, I came apart. Maybe it is the mother in me who grieves for his mom, maybe it is the abruptness in which I found out or maybe it is the sadness in realizing that he had so much to offer the world, his friends and family that will go unfinished. Whatever it was, my response surprised me. I found myself walking that fine line of grief. Do I remain stoic and strong so that my own child has someone to lean on (and really, who am I fooling with that thought?) Or do I show him the depth of my sorrow and hope he absorbs the truth: all mothers feel the loss when a child dies.

Sometimes I hate being a grown-up.

Chapter Twenty Nine

The Parenting Manual Needs a Job Description

The elusive universal "Parent Manual" leaves out a lot of important stuff when it comes to the job description for mother. For instance, it extols the joys of motherhood, explains the birth process and sets you up for day-to-day infant care with a fair amount of accuracy. But, when it comes to the less tangible "worry" section, . . .well, it falls flat. There is no tangible time line for when you might be "finished" with the parenting process - especially the worry. I figured it must be upon some specific event like graduation from college. The child has grown, become educated and is now ready to face the world on his own. Wow. Who was I kidding? With a kid who graduated into the worst economic crisis in our lifetime, I quickly learned that what really happens is that the worry just shifts because it still takes up the same amount of space, time and stomach aches.

Lucky for you guys, I realized long ago that as far as my friends go, age doesn't matter. At some point, everyone becomes my age-- great for the older friends, maybe not so great for the younger ones but that is beside the point. I am only bringing this up because I have a friend who just had her first child three weeks ago and that, coupled with the recent death of someone else's child, has thrown me into an introspective tizzy of which I simply MUST verbalize.

As I held this incredibly perfect, eight-pound bundle of beauty recently new to the world, I marveled at how her emergence has completely changed the priorities of her young parents. It doesn't matter how ready you BELIEVE you are, the moment the baby arrives you revel in the joys of a healthy poop, attune to the sound of steady breathing, and knowing from that time on you will do whatever it takes to ensure their child's life is all it can be. And sometimes those challenges are colossal.

I look at the women I am blessed to know and find that I stand in awe of what they do everyday in the name of motherhood without the slightest clue that what they do is admirable. It is simply part of the job.

I have a good friend who, just five months ago learned that her son is gay. When our children are born, we build dreams for them based on what our society has dubbed a "norm." He will grow up, become successful, fall in love, get married and have kids. All well and good if you aren't the mother of a gay child because all of those things certainly can happen, it just isn't how you have pictured it. And so, when after he had come out to his friends and the word started to spread, he came out to his mother without any real guarantee that she would accept it. Faced with this startling admission, this mom, who **never saw it coming** did the only natural thing she could do: she gathered her little boy into her arms and cried. Were they tears of grief? Sadness over what now would never be as she pictured? No, as she held her son in her arms she cried for the pain he had held to himself for the last two years and said a prayer of thanks that his painful secret had not driven him to do the unthinkable.

 We are not prepared, when we are learning Lamaze breathing, and focusing on the impending birth, for what that newborn will require when the care is lifelong. I have another friend whose oldest child was born with a myriad of disabilities. Recently, she spent a good week in the ICU because her now 23 year old son had been experiencing increasingly dangerous seizures. The idea being that when the next seizure of that sort occurred, it could be witnessed, recorded and then treated. The room was like a fishbowl with medical staff observing them at all hours. Her son's head was hooked and wired to transmitters and they simply lived their days out in that glass room HOPING for a dangerous seizure so that they could figure out how to manage them and move on. My friend never once complained, never once lamented that her own birthday was spent in that fishbowl and NEVER considered a pity party as an option. Instead, she jokingly referred to her situation with the cameras and infrared cameras, microphones and such as her own reality show...called... "Our Little Head Case!", all the while hoping for the dangerous seizure because that's what was needed to help him in the long run.

Another friend has a terrific son who, in his new-found freedom of college has found that sometimes there are consequences that are costly to say the least (and who among us hasn't been there?). And while she worries and frets over his choices, she knows in the end he will have to figure it out on his own. Let's face it, we can only hope the lessons we imparted to our progeny manifest themselves at some point and our children become happy, law-abiding adults. Pray for happy - stress law-abiding because that opens up a whole new sub chapter of worry.

Children are challenges. Although the caliber of challenge differs from child to child and sometimes the challenges we are presented with feel insurmountable, giving up is never an option. As mothers, we NEVER give up on our children. Last week a 21-year-old child died after fighting an insidious disease. His mother has had to face probably the most gut wrenching challenge one can face. After having her own stem cells harvested and transplanted to her son, she had to stand by while, in the end, it did not offer the miracle we had all hoped. Instead, she had to face that her child was going to die and support him through it until the end.

It's not in the Parent Manual. It's just what mother's do.

Chapter Thirty

To The Good Life

Those of you that know me know that I am a beach girl at heart. A body of water and a stretch of sand to enjoy it by and I'm good to go. So, it stands to reason, doesn't it, that when we retire, we are moving to the desert? Right? And not just any desert mind you, but a world famous, playground of the stars desert. . . Palm Springs, CA. And the truth is, I can't wait. In fact, we have taken a concrete step toward retirement by building a house there, amongst the mountains, deserts and movie stars and we are starting a road trip out there tomorrow.

When I turned that precarious age of aging, 40, Moondoggy had a midlife crisis and bought me a cute little white Mazda Miata for my birthday. Not a bad deal really. He didn't start spending long hours in the bars, he didn't dump me for a trophy wife (and really, why would he?) and he didn't succumb to one of the hundreds of emails telling him he had won millions in the Pan Asian/Ecuadoran lottery where he could collect said money for a minimal, yet healthy fee. All he did was go out a buy a sports car and give it to me. I couldn't lose! Somehow over the years, my treasured Miata managed to morph itself into a silver Porsche Boxster

becoming the icon for which Moondoggy equates
retirement bliss (although I will ALWAYS remind him
that it is, in fact, MINE.) And with a little over three
years until he waltzes out of the cloud factory for good,
we are beginning to move important stuff out to
California. . . like my car.

CHAPTER THIRTY ONE

GIDGET AND MOONDOGGY GO WEST
PART DEUX

I'll admit I'm not up on my Bible stories but I do recall something about plagues being visited upon our Earth. Locusts, wind, fire? Something like that. I don't know the actual malady or timeline there, but I can tell you during that decree, some higher up pointed to us, whispered an aside to the plague CEO and said, "Hey, I want to play a joke on those guys. Could you add water to the list and focus it specifically on the them?" And He did.

I was racing back from the train station after having dropped off Youngest Son who was heading back to college. Moondoggy was packing the car and we were set to begin our cross country journey. I called him to to tell him that Operation Child Drop-Off was complete when he uttered the dreaded words of which I am all too familiar, "Our basement flooded." He didn't have to say AGAIN, because, with us, that is a given.

Our water troubles started in Virginia with a sewage back-up not once, twice or even three times, but five times during our 18-month stay in the apartment. It followed us to Illinois where we experienced such everyday water issues as: Our first well did not have potable water and the well driller was forced by the state to dig us a new one after a 6-month battle; after the second well was dug, the first had to be rendered unusable so it was filled with concrete - which would have been great had it not flowed through the underground crevices and entered our new GOOD well and flowed through our pipes into the house; our second well tested bad for e coli after a 500-year flood that changed the water table causing us to install the "Ozonator" to treat the water. . .which exploded a few years later, knocking a valve on the hot water heater and flooding the basement. I could go on, but you get the idea.

So, I slowed down a little hoping I could waste time until Moondoggy had shut it down and cleaned up the mess - I know better than to walk in on one of his water clean-ups. I even pondered a stop at Victoria's Secret but was too anxious to start our road trip to think about cute panties.

Turns out I arrived in time to watch as Moondoggy sucked the last of the flood water into our trusty wet-vac thereby signaling that it was time to head west.

Funny thing. We may have chosen to head west to a warm, dry climate but let's not forget that it only takes one typo to turn west into wets!

Chapter Thirty Two

A Song For Every State

You might be asking yourself, "Hey Self, what do you suppose this great country looks like from the point of view a low-to-the-road convertible vehicle?" Well, I can answer that for you. If it's raining and you are driving your way through Missouri in a silver Porsche Boxster after the sun has gone down it can be quite spectacular.

I am convinced that there must have been a memo sent out to all folks living within view of the interstate directing them to decorate for Christmas. I am further convinced that there must have been a prize involved for as each mile passed, the light show intensified. Compound that with rain on the windshield fracturing the light into thousands more. . .and well, I am hard pressed for a worthy description. Suffice it to say, Missourians put the rest of us to shame and we should all rush out and buy more lights for our own displays immediately! I myself am drawn to the blue LED variety and am now stockpiling for next year.

After a shockingly good rest at a La Quinta Inn which is pet friendly (read FREE), has new beds and a hot breakfast in the morning. . .we headed into Oklahoma. I didn't actually experience the wind come sweepin' down the plain, because I was driving and a hard frost covered the top rendering it impossible to put down without cracking. . .not that I would have gone top down anyway, but one does think about it.

I don't like to brag, but I can sing. Seriously. And, what's more I am a spot-on mimic. So, with my ipod flowing through the car radio, I regaled Moondoggy with the likes of Patsy Cline, Janis Joplin, Frank Sinatra and Green Day (I am nothing if not eclectic!) I must have been pretty good too because when the ipod died, Moondoggy promised to see that it got charged for the next day. What a guy!

Yeah, about the ipod... he almost sounded sincere the next day when I plugged it in and found that it had not, in fact, been recharged. What's a girl to do? We were in Texas. I sang "Rose of San Antone" a cappella.

That'll teach him.

CHAPTER THIRTY THREE

RESOLVE THIS!

DON'T DO IT!!!!! That is my warning to anyone of you who believes they need to make some kind of silly promise to themselves just because the calendar year is moving up a notch. The New Year's Resolution? It's a hoax. And, it is designed by a secret society of fitness gurus, diet centers, and out-of-work shrinks who are really just trying to drum up business. I'm not kidding, I've seen the underbelly and it's NOT pretty.

The whole resolution idea may have been originally based on good and personal betterment, but it has morphed into a money grubbing race to see you fail. By far, the preponderance of resolutioners vow to lose weight and get into shape and the secret society knows this; mobilizing forces to act under names like Jenny Craig and Seattle Sutton. They will tell you they are your friends . . . for a price and you'll feel their love too . . . for awhile. You will lose weight. You will feel confident and then, they'll cut you loose, but it's not because they are proud or happy for you - OH NO. It's only after you have decided to go it on your own that they will turn to one another with that evil grin, nod their collective head and triumphantly high five because THEY KNOW YOU ARE GOING TO FAIL! That's right, they are marking their little Franklin Planners for your return next January where you will come back to lose the SAME 15 pounds again and gladly pay for their help AGAIN. So who wins here? Not you.

Local and chain gyms are the same. You join in January with gusto. You go everyday and work your body into a cardiac frenzy. And then, you hurt. You take a day off. It becomes a three-day-a-week proposition for awhile and then by March (the magic month of Spring Break) you are side tracked by something (usually a vacation) and by April, it's all over. You probably signed a year-long contract with that gym, but you don't care anymore. The weather is getting warm, baseball and beer season has begun and really? Who wants to be stuck in a gym when you can be outside? And what about Mr. Peak Fitness? Mr. Gold's Gym? He is counting his dollars knowing you'll re-sign, when? Next January. Cha Ching!

In the meantime, you'll notice more and more counseling centers putting out their shingles. "Do you feel like you can't follow through? Do you think you are out of control? Do you feel like a failure? Come talk to me because I can help you past this. You are a good person. You are lovable and capable. And for $150 for a

50-minute hour, I'll make sure you are back on track by . . . oh . . . next December."

I say don't resolve to make any change based on the calendar. And DON'T resolve to do something you've attempted before without permanent success. I, of course, resolved long ago to NEVER make another New Year's Resolution again and it's worked. Besides, I have trouble committing to anything farther than three days out. Making a lifetime commitment where I am solely responsible and have only to answer to myself ? I'd rather pull out my fingernails.

Chapter Thirty Four

When Reality Tastes Good

Every so often I am presented with a reality check - I usually don't ask for but one ,nevertheless, it is served up directly in my face. Some are easier to swallow, but others? Not so much.

I abhor math. The fact is, once my math skills advanced from add, subtract, multiply and divide; I was pretty much done. Fractions were my first stumbling block. I remember my dad trying to teach me fractions by using a hershey bar (no nuts!). He wanted to start with "half" as a concept. He handed me the chocolate and asked me to break the bar at the point I thought was half.

The whole lesson ended quickly when I decided "half" was all but a sliver, popped it in my mouth and walked away leaving him with nothing but a sliver of a Hershey bar and a shaking head. By the time they started replacing numbers with letters, I was trading the unknown integers for sappy poetry (I've read some of it lately and the gag effect is HUGE.) I abhor math; but that reality was very easy to swallow.

I can even make a case for another reality: I can't sing. Yes, in the past I have been known to declare my voice the next best thing to Streisand so I know most of you find that shocking beyond belief but, alas, it's true. I came to this realization in full and complete acceptance when I joined my church's choir. Let it be said that I have a four-note range, although I am not sure what those four notes are actually and as my friend Cindy kindly put it, " We are neither soprano, alto or bass. We are the puddin' part - just falling into any area that our voice is able." Cindy is painfully honest but she is usually right. Pudding? Yeah, I could swallow that reality check easily.

The one reality that completely confounded me and took me by total and utter surprise is this: I'm not tall. You're shocked, right? It's true and I didn't know this until I was in my late 30s or early 4's. I KNOW! This is how it went down but you need to know the history from where my delusion was spawned.

I started kindergarten, like most others, at the age of five but, unlike most others, was a full head taller. In fact, in kindergarten the only other kids my height were two girls: Connie and Joannie. And it went like that throughout my entire elementary school career. When picking teams in gym class, the first girls picked were always Connie, Joanie, and me, oh, and scrappy girl named Julie because she could probably have beat up any boy our age with one hand tie behind her back - blindfolded. And why were we always chosen first?

Because those boys equated tall with athletic. In my case, the boys were dumb. It didn't end there though, Connie and I were ALWAYS in the center of the back row of any school picture (and I have the yearbooks to prove it) and our "tallness" was constantly pointed out by boys who liked to stand next to us and pretend they were scared because we were "giants."

With my advanced height came an early puberty and all the glory events as well as the awkwardness that goes with it. Never a good time in any girl's life, add the pressure of everyone expecting you to act much older because you look much older and you start to believe your own PR. So, it is not with pride (except maybe a little because I just realized I have a wry smile on my face) that I was able to walk into a liquor store in Pennsylvania at age 14 and buy a bottle of Mad Dog 20/20 - for a friend, of course - and never raise the suspicion of the guy behind the counter. Between people who naturally treated me like I was older coupled with the constant reminder of my height at every turn, it was only natural that I felt tall.

My choir was practicing for our first Christmas cantata and we were in the process of getting lined up on the risers. I didn't really notice that anything looked uneven or just plain wrong when my painfully honest BFF Cindy asked, " Judi, what are you doing?" I looked around and told her in my "duh" voice, "Lining up." I looked around me and realized I was standing amongst several men who ranged from 5' 11" - 6' 10" (yes, I said 6' 10") and they were all looking down on me. I stepped down a row and started to settle in when I saw BFF Cindy shaking her head and pointing down to the next row. I sighed and stepped down again and she leaned over and whispered, " What were you doing?" I whispered back, "Lining up by height." I can't describe the decibel of Cindy's shriek but suffice it to say had it been a TV comedy gag, it would have been a full on spit take followed by peels of giggles as she loudly asked, "Who EVER told you that you are tall???????"

Needless to say, swallowing that reality has been difficult but it has produced an epiphany. When reality comes in the form of a Hershey bar or pudding, I gladly swallow it - which may explain why my weight doesn't match my height as well as I thought it did.

CHAPTER THIRTY FIVE

AND HE RAN AWAY TO JOINED THE CIRCUS

I have spoken often of the plethora of famous people that hale from my part of Michigan. . .until someone tells me to shut up. There are, however, several people from the northern Illinois area who have gone on to become famous, as well. There's Joan Allen, Michele Williams of TLC, William Katz and of course THE Jeremy Smith. Who? You know, the kid who ran away with the circus.

A few years ago Moondoggy came home from work with a story about a co-worker's kid. This kid had been a champion diver and gymnast in the county and was recognized by some pretty impressive people. But, as Moondoggy tells the story, . . ."Jeremy up and joined the circus at 16."

"And his parents were OK with this?" I ask incredulously. "I guess so, Smith was talking about it today. Said they pay him pretty well and pay for his housing. I guess it's a pretty well-known circus. "

I imagined Jeremy as one of the flying trapeze guys - living in a small trailer behind the elephants and really, I wondered what in the world his parents were thinking. The circus? I am a former carnie (another book altogether!) and I know there are just too many diseases you can catch on the road with, well, clowns. But who I am to judge? My parents let me work in carnivals one summer.

Months - maybe years pass and Moondoggy again comes home and says, "Remember when I told you about Jeremy Smith joining the circus? Well, they are coming back to the states to open a show here. "

Hmmmmm, I think. A circus that has been traveling out of the country. A well-known circus. They pay well. I can add 2+2+2 and get 6 so I ask, "What is the name of this circus?"

"I dunno, " Moondoggy shrugs, "something foreign I think."

"Something foreign like Cirque du Soliel by any chance?" I ask.
He snaps his fingers, "Yeah, that's it!"
"And they are opening a permanent show in Las Vegas, right?"
"Yeah," Moondoggy says, "How do you know?"
BECAUSE IT'S FREAKIN CIRQUE DU SOLIEL not some rinky dink traveling circus. Homer Simpson forehead slap and required, "DOH!"

So Jeremy is one of the leads in, "KA", in Vegas and we are headed there this weekend to see the show. Afterward, we are meeting Jeremy and he is giving us a back stage tour. I don't want to be a name dropper - Tom Cruise - but many celebrities attend the later show and go back stage afterward to meet the performers. I'm not saying that all those celebs will be clamoring to have their pictures taken with me, but rest assured, I will be lurking in the background of any and all photos where celebrities gather so look for me on E! Or not.

Chapter Thirty Six

Vegas? I'd Rather Run Away With The Circus

There isn't anything that can be written about Las Vegas that hasn't been written already. Except maybe this - I hate Las Vegas. I don't just hate Las Vegas, I loathe it. Crowds that aimlessly mill about staring gape mouthed at the Eiffel Tower, the statue of Liberty and the Great Pyramid of Giza all in a one square block; blue haired ladies with red lipstick and a cigarette dangling from their lips as they play the penny slots; and the constant reverberation of bells ringing, machines beeping and horns honking assaulting my ears are only part of the problem. Apparently, I no longer consider losing money a form of entertainment. And really? I've seen some Vegas shows that have left me totally underwhelmed. So what is the draw?

I'm can't be positive but the phrase, "What happens in Vegas, stays in Vegas," must have more to do with the amount of money a person can drop simply by walking down the street than the knowing eye-wink followed by bad behavior that the tourism council would have you believe.

It used to be you could enjoy a decent buffet meal at any of the casinos for $4.99 - the idea being, you eat quick and cheap and get back in the casino. Now that they have promoted the whole "family friendly" angle, they have upped the prices and included all sorts of thrills for those smart enough not to gamble but not smart enough to realize that $15 for a roller coaster ride that lasts two minutes is still a losing proposition.

And why are the only chairs for sitting and resting located in front of slot machines? As usual, I digress. The reason for our visit was to see the Cirque Du Soleil show, "KA."

As you may recall, we were there to see Jeremy Smith perform in the show. Following the spectacular, we were to be afforded the privilege of a personal back stage tour given by Jeremy himself. Well, if it weren't for bad luck, then we would have no luck at all. The weekend we were there was the weekend of the Oscars which equals a theater with no celebrities. Ok, I can handle that, I'm really there to see the show not see celebrities see the show. Then, we get a call from Jeremy's father. Jeremy is ill, he hasn't missed a show in 5 years but he is not going to be appearing. However, he arranged for his girlfriend, another artist and one of the main stars of the show, to meet us and give us a tour.

Holy Schnikes! The show itself is beyond any description I can offer. To try would render it just adequate. The stage is mobile and is often set vertical, perpendicular to the floor and the performers flip, dance and fly up and down the thing. There is a story that is sometimes difficult to follow only because I was so mesmerized by the action, I lost myself in the moment. If Vegas is sensory overload in the worst way, KA is sensory orgasm (yeah, I said it.)

Afterward, we met Jeremy's girlfriend and her sister at the door and she took us backstage. She plays one of the main characters in KA and she is positively diminutive. I mean so tiny that if I were a few inches shorter and weighed a lot less I would still look like an oaf next to her. What she may lack in stature is made up in remarkable talent, vast backstage knowledge and kindness. She explained how the stage moved, how the costumes are stored and how much the wigs cost (5 freakin' digits.) She explained some of the moves that Jeremy performs and showed us the dressing rooms. She did all of this at 11:30 p.m. for people she had never met and would probably never see again while all of the other performers were changing and rushing home to begin their "weekends."

And that, the whole Cirque experience, erased the fact that I smoked 2 packs of cigarettes just by breathing, collected a card decks worth of call girl cards on the street, and lost $20 in a slot machine. Cirque Du Soleil? YES! Vegas? Meh.

CHAPTER THIRTY SEVEN
JUST WHEN I THINK IT'S ALL ABOUT ME

I have two phenomenal children. I am always amazed at what they accomplish and, quite frankly, that I didn't ruin them somehow in the growing up process. That being said, I can now tell you that I once uttered the following words with tearful emotion and utter conviction . . ." He's everything to me." I was talking to my sister and I was talking about my dog. And, well, it's kind of true. My boys are great but they don't sit on my lap anymore, they don't want to go out for walks to the park or play with me and they don't really listen to me at all. Moose does. He follows me from room to room ready to do anything to please me. He cries when I leave and jumps for joy when I return. He also brings me lots of attention out in public. What more could a girl ask for?

Last Tuesday, I took the brave and somewhat nerve wracking step of flying Moose across country. I bought the soft sided pet carrier approved by all airlines and paid the extra $100 to allow him to fly in the cabin with me and headed for the gate. There I was bustling down the American Airlines terminal with my new very cool black leather travel bag that contained my important worldly possessions such as my wallet, my Kindle and my eyelash curler (oh and my phone.) Clutching dog treats, and baggies in one hand, leash and dog in the other garnering "ooohs and ahhs" from passersby, I made my way to gate K8. I felt positively royal. My dog is really cute especially when he has been recently bathed and brushed and I could hear the conversations started in the name of my Moose.

When we got to the gate, my phone dinged, indicating a text message so I picked Moose up, tucked him under my arm and checked my phone. People text me a lot because I am so important. Now, I am no stranger to being mistaken for someone else, I mean the resemblance between me and Paris Hilton is uncanny especially when we are both holding small dogs in our arms and texting while in an airport. Apparently people feel the need to inquire. I heard the voice quietly at first but because I can barely see the letters on my phone without glasses, I was concentrating pretty heavily on my text response and tuned out the voice. I heard it again a little louder, "Excuse me. EXCUSE ME? I hate to bother you while you are busy . . . ." Oh yeah, she clearly thought I was a celebrity. I thought about completely ignoring her in Paris Hilton fashion but that seemed too harsh a non acknowledgement so I turned to face the voice. She smiled, "How ADORABLE! Does she bite?" Why is that always the first question? All dogs are capable of biting unless their teeth have fallen out or been removed. "No," I replied and he started panting and wagging his fluffy white tail. She reached out and scratched behind his ears, "She's very sweet." Ok, my gut was telling me to say, "It's a HE," but instead I smiled and thanked her and then I couldn't keep my mouth shut and I said, " But he's a boy." The lady stepped back and looked at the ground, " Oh well," she said, " I was going to tell you that she had a little accident when you picked her up but you were so busy texting I decided to wait and now you are standing in a big ol' pile of HIS crap." She turned and walked away.

I'll bet that never happens to Paris Hilton.
And ok, my children never would have done that in the airport so maybe the dog love isn't quite as satisfying as kids even if they are grown and gone. . .but it's close!

Chapter Thirty Eight

And I Thought It Was About The Flip Flops!

I call this life my nutshell and here is one of the reasons why. This is a real and true story of how I was pedually (and you'll get what this means by the time the story is through) assaulted one afternoon in Hobby Lobby. Yes! Freakin' Hobby Lobby.

Growing up, your parents warn you to be wary of strangers. They teach you what is appropriate behavior from people you know and they guide you through the growing years leaving you with kernels of wisdom, tools to protect yourself and hopefully the common sense to know when something ain't right.

So where was my weirdo radar the day I walked into Hobby Lobby? It was a sunny day in spring - one of those first warm days where a cute skirt and flip flops feel, well, right. I was just starting to wear regular shoes after an achilles surgery that left a scar on the back of my right foot that resembled a four inch scorpion. I had just enjoyed my first pedicure in eight months and with the shedding of a fat cast and then the walking boot, I could see my ankles on BOTH feet and they looked darn cute! I felt positively sensual with those pretty pink toes, my sea foam green flip flops and both ankles exposed.

I was minding my own business in the decorative paper aisle just looking at the vast array of colors and patterns and gushing over the possibilities. Yes, I'm weird like that. I should have been paying better attention to my surroundings though because this is what happened next: A guy, probably in his early 20s slowly follows me from aisle one to aisle two. . .the scrapbooking aisle. Yeah, where were my warning bells? What's a guy doing in the scrapbooking aisle? Maybe, I thought, he works here. Yeah, I liked that explanation. He sweeps up the aisle behind me and then back down next to me when he very politely says, "Excuse me." I look up and he is standing very close, "May I ask where you got your shoes?" I look down at my sea foam green flip flops and quite frankly I'm thinking , "These? Really?" but I answer, "Payless." And before I can ask why, I see he has his camera phone focused on my left foot and he takes a picture and then RUNS, almost knocking me into a rack of embellishments in the process.

I was stunned. What just happened? It actually took me a few seconds to register the oddness of the whole thing. Was my flip flop that beautiful? Did my toe nail polish intrigue him? Does he have a foot fetish? Oh Lord, did he just take a picture of my foot? What's he going to do with it? Is he, oh no, OH NO, is he going to post it on some freak site on the internet? Holy Cats! Have I just been assaulted?

I went to the manager and told him about my pedual assault. I thought the guy might laugh (I mean let's face it, it is pretty funny) but NO! The man goes ballistic. Locks down the store and conducts a thorough search while another employee stands protective guard over me. No perp. So, flanked by the manager on one side and an employee on the other, I was escorted to my car while scanning the parking lot for the creep. I asked the manager - given the way he handled it - if this had happened before and he looked at me like I was crazy, "No, but,"and he looked down at my foot with the scorpion scar," but taking a picture of THAT is just gross." Thanks buddy, but it was the other foot.

I never did do a web search to see if my foot ever showed up somewhere on the internet. Quite frankly, I don't want to know. But, between you and me, if it did end up somewhere I don't want to think about, I take comfort in the knowledge that at least it was my good foot!

Chapter Thirty Nine

The Vodka Option

I was in my fourth day of a self-imposed exile. The reason for my withdrawal from the hubbub of the day-to-day activity of the human race begins with an end. The end of that story goes something like this:

And the pasta with artichoke hearts and garlic was simply sublime. So delicious was my meal that I was rendered incapable of putting my fork down until I had consumed every last morsel of shrimp (four of them), artichoke hearts (seven of them) and roasted cloves of garlic (28 of them.)

You get the picture. I ate 28 cloves of garlic. And I'm not saying I didn't enjoy every last bite, I did – and I have been enjoying it over and over again since last Tuesday. It never occurred to me, during my repast that the garlic would permeate my digestive tract and try escaping from every available body opening possible, but it did.

It was a long weekend get-a-way with my sister to a charming Bed & Breakfast on Mackinac Island. We hadn't seen each other in over two years and we decided to celebrate, as sisters do, with a big 'ol artery clogging meal. It never occurred to me that would be a bad idea.

My first clue manifested itself in the middle of the night when my sister – who was sharing a hotel room with me – threw open the windows even though the wind was howling and the rain was falling in horizontal sheets. I asked her what was wrong and she asked if I could maybe stop breathing for awhile, like the rest of the night.

It was no better in the morning and in fact, had seeped out the pores of my skin and into the linens on my bed. I'm sure the staff was happy when I checked out that morning and my sister did not linger in a long goodbye – that's kinda hard to do between holding your breathe and trying to gulp fresh air.

The next morning, I got online and Googled , "how to get rid of garlic smell." There are exactly 104,000 sites giving detailed, foolproof, methods for eliminating garlic breath. . .I chose the first reasonable method.

Vodka.

Seriously, the site suggested that vodka would not only neutralize the internal garlic odor, it would also kill the residual odor on my breath. Sounded logical to me and then I had an epiphany. When a pet has a run-in with a skunk, what do you bath the pet in? Tomato juice! This was fast becoming a method that sounded like it actually might be fun. I had the juice, and I had the vodka, it was morning making it the perfect time for a stiff Bloody Mary. So, on a Thursday morning, all by myself, I mixed a strong cocktail and drank it down fast. I drank it fast because it was meant to be medicinal, not a true cocktail. I mean if I had enjoyed it like a cocktail there by myself on a Thursday morning, I would have cause to consider a 12 step program so by drinking it fast.- like I would a dose of Nyquil, I could justify the whole thing without social repercussions. Or so I thought. Guess what. If you drink - no GULP a stiff Bloody Mary to avoid the connotations attached to drinking in the morning, I assure you it will manifest in a more obvious manner and it will do so instantly.(Note to self and to friends: Do not Facebook with people while drinking. . .alone. . .in the morning. My apologies to anyone I may have offended.)

After consuming the vodka I thought it would be a good idea to respond to a letter to the editor of our local paper that had got me thinking. It was about, um, it was about, well, it was about something really pressing here in our thriving Metroplis anyway and I was sure MY opinion would surely convince the town to see otherwise. I was eloquent, adamant and completely blotto.

I woke to the phone ringing around one in the afternoon and blindly grasped it before the answering machine picked up. It was my sister. I explained that I was currently nursing a hangover from a morning drunk that was merely an honest effort to get rid of the garlic. "So THAT explains the email. Did it work?" she asked.

Judging by the way my dog hid his nose under the pillow, I'd say no. "What email?" I asked.

"The email I received this morning where you blame the decline in quality curriculum as well as the entire recession on the death of Princess Diana and suggest if we all travel to England to tell the Queen that if her son had been a nicer person, none of this would have ever happened. You said he wasn't even as good looking as Prince Andrew which made the whole debacle a huge disappointment because then we could have, at least, had a reason to root for him. And, it goes on. I won't even mention what you said about Camilla Parker Bowles and Princess Margaret but it wasn't pretty," Thank goodness I only sent it to her. I think. I hope. I wonder if I used the words "horse-face" or "horse" at all. Then I wondered if I had spelled either of them with a "wh" instead.

That Thursday was kind of a lost day. And FYI – it takes a full week for 28 cloves of garlic to work through the average human body with or without the vodka option.

Chapter Thirty Forty

I'm Not a Doctor But I'm Usually Right

Have I mentioned that I am a beach girl at heart? Drag me anywhere on this earth, force me to climb a mountain or zip-line through a rainforest but do not, I repeat, DO NOT get in the way of my every other year week at the beach. That would be a deal breaker in my book. I look forward to this week from the moment we leave the beach, until the next time we go. My children feel the same way – drag them anywhere, but give them the beach every other year. If Matthew McConaughy were to ring me up and pledge his undying love to me wanting me to meet him in Malibu to seal the deal, I'd say, "No can do, Babe. Wrong beach, but me and Moondoggy are headed to my beach if you want to hang there." Stop it - I would too.

So, when Moondoggy mentioned that his stomach hurt four days before we were set to leave for my beloved beach vacation, even HE dismissed it as a pulled muscle. However, as the days moved forward, the pain came and went and came again – worsening just a bit each time. Finally, on Thursday (the day before beach departure), he went to the doctor who thought perhaps he was developing an ulcer and scheduled a CT scan for the next morning. Our departure would be put off by a few hours. I pouted but put my selfishness aside for my beloved Moondoggy. Thursday evening the pain worsened and Moondoggy pondered the notion of calling the doctor back. Pondered? My dialing the number and shoving the phone into his hand should have been a big clue as to how I felt. I'm not a doctor but I now believed it was his appendix and I had a schedule to keep. The doctor told him to go immediately to the ER – which we did and five hours later (1:30 a.m.) he was wheeled into a room sporting a lovely four inch incision with seven staples and he was minus one appendix (ahem. . .who was right?)

As I've already said, and as Moondoggy had astutely pointed out (ad nauseum), I am not a doctor but I knew there was another disease lurking around in that hospital room, even with the offending appendix removed, and I had to invoke it's name: Vacationus Cancelitis. This would be a long and painful disease that would inflict heavy and repeated bouts of agony for anyone around me for at least the next two years. The prognosis isn't good. Trust me.   I did *graciously* suggest we cancel so that Moondoggy could recover at home the next week – but he graciously suggested the rest of us go to the beach and leave him. I tried not to squeal too loudly but I was willing to jump at that chance. Because my friend Cindy is a nurse and our friend meter was reading full, I felt a minimal amount of guilt as oldest son and I eagerly mapped out our route while Moondoggy slipped in and out of sleep in his hospital bed. Then. . . I spoke with the surgeon about our travel dilemma and, guess what!   He surprisingly said *Moondoggy could go* as long as he was comfortable in the car! Woo Hoo! New plan.

I wheeled up to the hospital around noon on Saturday tooting the horn, ready to get the show on the road. With the Jeep fully packed; coolers full, blankets, pillows and ipods, I got a lesson from the doc on how to remove staples (which would need to be done in a week and looked awfully fun to do), settled the patient into the passenger seat with a blanket and pillow and shoved massive pain killers down his throat. He doesn't remember much of the trip except the part where I removed his staples. Did you know that if this is done on the left side instead of the right, it causes severe pain? Me either. But I know now. Anyway, I had a humdinger of a time and tell him he did too, and really that's all that counts.

That's not wrong. Is it?

Chapter Forty One

What a Girl Wants. . .What a Girl Needs

It's an old story. Good girl falls for bad boy (and secretly believes that she can "change" him) and then he defaults to his nature and BAM! Good girl has another broken heart.

A friend of mine has a daughter who has repeated this pattern time and time again with boyfriends named, Shithead, Loser, Lazy Ass and Lacks Earning Potential. . .at least those are the names her mother has used. After the last break-up (where mother secretly pops the cork on some bubbly and thanks God) I told her straight up exactly what her daughter needs. A gay man.

I am serious. There is nothing better for a woman's fragile heart than a gay man and that is the real and true fact of it. Here's why: A gay man will make a woman feel like a queen. He is polite, he is caring, he identifies with her woes, he will make her laugh and laugh with her and he will never ask for any physical pleasure in return. Once a girl establishes a friendship with a gay man, she will begin to recognize the qualities she is looking for in her very own male and adjust her internal compass. At least that is the hope.

The next step is a dog.

And that is when I had my own personal epiphany regarding my own personal situation. It's time for me to come out of the closet. I have three good men in my life and I have waxed poetic on their good qualities but, sadly, they don't speak female. So, I have my dog to fill the gaps. Even better than that? I hit the Daily Double because. . . my dog is gay.

I put the whole puzzle together only recently. Moose is a Bichon Frise, a rather pretentious name for a 12 lb. pup, but perfectly describes his appearance. My dog is soft, fluffy and white. He requires constant grooming that includes frequent blow dry and comb outs. Further, my dog knows he looks good so he gets a little testy when a matte begins to form and he insists I get rid of it. This usually entails him boring his dark brown eyes into me and stamping his paw when I don't respond. He demands attention from time to time but who doesn't? His collar of choice is black leather with metal studs. You get the picture.

Apart from his appearance, my dog has displayed a certain predilection for male dogs. Not just any male dog, mind you, but a beautiful specimen of Bichon Frise who is perhaps not the brightest bulb in the pack. Henry lives with my good friend Darling Deb and her family that includes four men and another male Bichon, Georgie. When Moose gets together with Henry and Georgie after the initial buzz around the house, Moose and Henry begin their dance of coy games like bait and switch to steal the toy, grooming each other around the head and neck and finally, well, Moose makes THE advance to which Darling Deb and I want to yell, "Get a room you guys!!!!" The thing is, Moose doesn't do this with Georgie at all and I think I know why. Georgie and Moose have the same father and I think Moose realizes that. There are certain lines you just don't cross no matter what you are.

Moose makes me feel like a queen. He loves nothing more than to spend time with me. He knows when I am sad and snuggles in right beside me. He prances when I am happy and doesn't ask for more than to love me and look good -- oh and if he had his way, he'd spell his name Mousse, but I nixed that. What more can I ask for, right?

A gay man is a girl's broken heart's best friend. A dog is a girl's best friend. I have a gay dog. So how lucky am I?

Chapter Forty Two

The Truth of it All

I spend a lot of time in California. And invariably when people hear that I am again boarding a plane west to sunny California, people genuinely ask me why I like it there so much. I tell them about my vitamin D deficiency but know that nobody buys that anymore. Well, here's the deal. Palm Springs is about as close to paradise as I can get without an ocean involved. Have I mentioned that I am a beach girl forward , backward and inside out? It's in my blood. And, there was a time when Moondoggy and I considered a permanent home on my beach in Virginia for when we retire. The problem is this, there is simply too much risk in ocean front property - like it can be there one day and one hurricane later, it can be gone. Winter is another problem. You can't exactly go sit out on the beach in Virginia in the winter time and you certainly can't go for a swim.

Our alternative was Palm Springs, California. Where else can you have a mountain view, warm days, sunshine all year and palm trees ? Seriously when it's cold and rainy in L.A. a quick trip over the mountains brings you to the desert where it is warm and sunny. The desert you say? Dry? Brown? Desolate. Well

here's a big ol' secret for you - Palm Springs and the
entire desert valley is like one big lush green oasis.
There are flowers blooming all year, groves of fruit trees
at your doorstep, pools and movie stars. I maintain that
when you come out on the desert side of the mountain
or step off the plane in Palm Springs, you pass through
a time warp where suddenly nothing is so all fired
important that it must get done immediately - maybe
after a golf game or some pool time. Happy hour starts
at 3 p.m. and lasts all year. Dining outside is de rigor
and dogs are allowed everywhere, EVERYWHERE as long
as they are leashed. My dog particularly enjoys a trip to
Home Depot. What would you expect from a dog named
Moose? Oh, I forgot, I outted him already.

When I get out there, I have food cravings that consist
of fresh fruit, grilled foods and hummus. When I get
there, I rarely watch TV, opting instead to sit out on the
verandah and read or write or listen to music. When I
am there, I hike through mountains and ride my bike all
over the place. When I am there, I go to the spa for a
pedicure where they offer me champagne, cookies and
spring water and they don't chat because they know I'm
in the zone. When I am there, I feel like a true grown-
up because there is no one to stand in judgment of what
I do, there is no one to loathe, there is no one to look
after but me.

I have someone who watches the house when I am
gone, I have someone who comes in to clean before I
arrive and I have a gardener that looks after the yard.

In short, how could this be wrong when a guy named Jesus mows my lawn? It's paradise, after all.

CHAPTER FORTY THREE

DOES IT ALL COMES DOWN TO THIS?

I have to wonder what my life has come to when I engage in the following conversation and don't realize the absurdity of it all until hours later.

It's Saturday. The sun came out. Those two things equal the desire to get up out of my red chair and get out of the house. Ditto for Moondoggy except he doesn't sit in the red chair. He sits in his room downstairs with the desk, fax machine, computer and bill book and plays office (he really HATES it when I say that!)

So we get in the car and head to Rockford along scenic Highway 2 that takes us along the Rock River with nothing between our Metropolis and Rockford but woods, fields, some houses, the river and a country and western bar. I need to go to Ulta3 for wrinkle cream and he needs to go to some man store for a battery charger. We pass a spot that hugs the river closely and there are about 10 ducks sitting in the snow. A good minute passes and this is what follows:

"Do you ever wonder how those little ducks can tolerate sitting in the snow for such long periods of time?" Moondoggy is grimacing as he poses the question, "I mean I don't care how much body fat it might have, it still has got to be miserable." I see that he is serious and it gets me to thinking because he's got a point. If I dislike the cold, Moondoggy loathes it.

"I worry about the poor horses in the pasture when we've had a good snow or really, the deer. Just look at the woods, they have little food to eat in the winter, no warm place to hunker down, and no foliage to protect them from hunters. If I was a deer, I'd move to Florida."

I've clearly given this some thought and, in fact, would have commented on the wild turkeys in the corn field too but the truth is, they aren't terribly bright.

Moondoggy shakes his head, "Naw, there's alligators in Florida," he says.
I rethink, "Ok, Arkansas. Are there alligators in Arkansas?"
"Worse," Moondoggy replies, "there's Arkansans."
I purse my lips; I thought we were being serious here.
"Maybe," he says, "they should move west but then there are cougars and mountain lions to contend with out there."
"No," I say,"the cougars there aren't after deer, they're after beefcake," I made a joke.
That produces a rye smile from Moondoggy. I notice something in my peripheral vision that I am quite sure is one of the bald eagles that like to cruise along the river in search of fish. I turn to gaze upon said eagle when I

realize it is really a low flying, slow gliding UPS jet. I
laugh and point it out to Moondoggy.
"Huh," he says, "We don't see many of those during the
day."
I nod my head in agreement, "No, we really don't."
"Gee,' says he, "I hope it's not rabid."

Now I ask you, what is more pathetic. . .that I
participated in this conversation or that it made perfect
sense to me?

One Long Thank You Note

My mother was a stickler for proper etiquette. We dressed for holiday meals, we never went anywhere if we were not invited, and we greeted my parent's friends, always calling them, "Mr. and Mrs." -which I still do. I cannot, for the life of me, bring myself to call some of the longest standing family friends by their first names. My mother was a paper snob and was never more adamant about it than when I got married. My wedding invitations were properly engraved on *Cranes* paper with the watermark in the proper spot. And she was a "Thank You" note slave driver. I used to write a great "Thank You" note. . .but it's been while.

It only took me 48 years to make the leap from the present tense of "writing a book" to the past tense of "wrote." That could not have happened without every single person who told me to do it. And really, sometimes, you have to create your own reality because others can suggest it but they aren't going to do it for you.

Thank you to my whole family, both here and no longer here. Each of you have been a profound influence in your encouragement and subject matter.

Thank you to my friends. You know who you are. If I have laughed, cried or gotten drunk with you, you are a friend.

Thank you to my "beach" sisters who have been my reading guinea pigs for years and will soon become subject matter too!

And finally, in this whole process, I learned the value of a good editor. Without the wicked and anal eye of my editor, I would still be floundering in a shallow puddle. Believe me, every single word, phrase and COMMA has been scrutinized through her filter thus, making me a much better writer. Thank you Ginger!

Judi Coltman has written for several regional and national publications in the realms of marketing, travel, and nuclear power. Coltman has also penned a few pieces of children's fiction - none of them published. . .yet. Currently she writes a blog entitled, "My Life in a Nutshell," www.jcoltman.blogspot.com where she injects her quirky sense of humor on daily life.

Coltman and her husband split time between their homes in Illinois and California. . .sometimes their paths even cross.